WJEC EDUQAS
THE POETRY ANTHOLOGY AND UNSEEN POETRY – THE COMPLETE ESSAY WRITING GUIDE

ANTHONY WALKER-COOK

First published in 2023 by Accolade Tuition Ltd
71-75 Shelton Street
Covent Garden
London WC2H 9JQ
www.accoladetuition.com
info@accoladetuition.com

Copyright © 2023 by Anthony Walker-Cook

The right of Anthony Walker-Cook to be identified as the author of this work has been asserted by him in accordance with the Copyright, Designs and Patents Act 1988.

All rights reserved. No part of this book may be reproduced in any form or by any electronic or mechanical means, including information storage and retrieval systems, without written permission from the author, except for the use of brief quotations in a book review.

Image, Page 17 ('Armitage in 2009') Copyright © Alexander Williamson. Licensed under CC BY 2.0: https://creativecommons.org/licenses/by/2.0/legalcode.
Source: https://www.flickr.com/photos/alexanderwilliamson/3768056245/

Image, Page 53 ('Carol Ann Duffy at Humber Mouth 2009') Copyright © Walnut Whippet. Licensed under CC BY 2.0.
Source: https://www.flickr.com/photos/walnutwhippet/3646825708/

ISBN 978-1-913988-33-3

FIRST EDITION
1 3 5 7 9 10 8 6 4 2

CONTENTS

Editor's Foreword — v
Introduction — xiii

THE POETRY ANTHOLOGY

Pairing I: War — 3
'Dulce Et Decorum Est' & 'The Manhunt'

Pairing II: Death — 19
'A Wife in London' & 'Mametz Wood'

Pairing III: Love — 35
'Sonnet 43' & 'The Soldier'

Pairing IV: Relationships — 49
'Valentine' & 'She Walks in Beauty'

Pairing V: Marriage — 63
'Cozy Apologia' & 'Afternoons'

Pairing VI: Innocence — 77
'The Prelude' & 'Death of a Naturalist'

Pairing VII: Place — 91
'London' & 'Living Space'

Pairing VIII: Nature — 103
'As Imperceptibly as Grief' & 'To Autumn'

Pairing IV: Power — 119
'Ozymandias' & 'Hawk Roosting'

UNSEEN POETRY

Pairing I: Dreams — 133
Pairing II: Loss/Sadness/Isolation — 147
Pairing III: London — 159
Pairing IV: Books and Reading — 171

Notes — 183

EDITOR'S FOREWORD

In your GCSE English Literature exam, you will be required to tackle four questions on poetry.

First off, you will be asked to tackle two questions relating to the poetry anthology you have been studying in school: one shorter question (worth 15 marks) that revolves around a single poem from the anthology chosen by the examiner; and one longer question (worth 25 marks) that requires you to compare the examiner-selected poem with another from the anthology of your choosing. (These two questions appear in the same paper as the Shakespeare assessment).

Your next two poetry questions will appear in a second paper, and these ones require students to engage with unseen poetry – that is, poems chosen by the examiner that students will *not* have studied in school. Again, there is a shorter question (worth 15 marks) that focuses on just one poem in isolation, and a longer question (worth 25 marks) that requires the student to compare the original poem with a second unseen poem. (These two questions appear in the exam paper that also contains questions on a post-1914 text and a 19th century novel).

When taken together, these four poetry questions represent 40% of your entire GCSE (anthology responses make up 20% of your grade, and unseen poetry responses make up another 20%). With this in mind, this guide is split into two parts. First, we will be dealing with two poetry anthology questions. Next, we will be tackling the two unseen poetry questions.

To be clear, this study guide is *not* intended to walk you through the anthology's poems line-by-line: there are great guides out there that do just that. No, this guide, by sifting through a series of mock exam questions, will demonstrate how to organise responses thematically and thus write stellar essays: a skill we believe no other study guide adequately covers!

A statue of the Ancient Greek poet Homer: the author of *The Odyssey* and *The Iliad*, and generally considered the granddaddy of Western poetry!

The Thematic Method

What do I mean by organising a response thematically?

Well, I have encountered students who have structured essays all sorts of ways: some who'll write about a text strictly chronologically, and others who'll give each language technique they spot its own paragraph. The method I'm advocating, on the other hand, involves picking themes (two for the smaller essays; three for the longer ones) that will allow you to holistically answer the question: these two to three themes will become the two to three content paragraphs of your essay, cushioned between a brief introduction and conclusion. Ideally, these themes will follow from one to the next to create a flowing argument. Within each of these thematic paragraphs, you can then ensure you are jumping through the mark scheme's hoops.

So to break things down further, each thematic paragraph will include various point-scoring components.

In the shorter 15 mark essays, each paragraph will include quotes from the text, offer analyses of these quotes, and discuss how they illustrate the theme you're discussing. In the longer, 25 mark essay, each paragraph will quote from the poem the exam board has set, offer analyses of these quotes, then discuss how the specific language techniques you have identified illustrate the theme you're discussing. In each paragraph, you will then quote from the second poem (the one you've chosen to write on from the anthology / the second unseen poem), and, while analysing these quotes and remarking on language techniques, also explain not only how the second poem relates to the chosen theme, but also how it does so differently (or not!) from the first poem.

Moreover, in your two poetry anthology essays, you will also need to incorporate into almost every paragraph some comment on the context in which the poetry was written (perhaps a detail about an author's life, perhaps an observation on the wider historical era) and how this helps us to understand the chosen theme.

Don't worry if this all feels daunting. Throughout this guide, Anthony (the very talented author of this volume) will be illustrating in great detail – by means of examples – how to build essays of this kind.

The beauty of the thematic approach is that, once you have your themes, you suddenly have a direction and a trajectory, and this makes essay writing a whole lot easier. However, it must also be noted that selecting themes in the first place is something students often find tricky. I have come across many candidates who understand poems inside out; but when they are presented with questions under exam conditions, and the pressure kicks in, they find it tough to break their response down into themes. The fact of the matter is: the process is a creative one and the best themes require a bit of imagination.

In this guide, Anthony shall take different exam-style questions, and shall put together a plan for each – a plan that illustrates in detail how we will be satisfying the mark scheme's criteria. Please do keep in mind that, when operating under timed conditions, your plans will necessarily be less detailed than those that appear in this volume. Rather, Anthony's responses (especially those for the longer, 25 mark questions) are designed to be as comprehensive as possible. ·

A photo of World War One soldiers, taken in Merville, France. Two of the anthology's poems – Wilfred Owen's 'Dulce Et Decorum Est' & Rupert Brooke's 'The Soldier' – deal with the First World War.

Before we move forward in earnest, I believe it to be worthwhile to run through the four Assessment Objectives the exam board associate with poetry responses – if only to demonstrate how effective the thematic response can be.

I would argue that the first Assessment Objective (AO1) – the one that wants candidates to 'read, understand and respond to texts' – will be wholly satisfied by selecting strong themes, then fleshing them out with quotes. Indeed, when it comes to identifying the top scoring candidates for AO1, the mark scheme explicitly tells examiners to look for responses that 'convey ideas with consistent coherence' and 'show a perceptive understanding', while making 'pertinent, direct references from across the text' – the word 'idea' is a synonym of theme, and 'pertinent, direct references' simply refers to quotes that appropriately support the theme you've chosen.

The second Assessment Objective (AO2) asks students to 'analyse the language, form and structure used by a writer to create meanings and effects, using relevant subject terminology where appropriate.' As noted, you will already be quoting from the poems as you back up your themes, and it is a natural progression to then analyse the language techniques used. In fact, this is far more effective than simply observing language techniques (personification here, alliteration there), because by discussing how the language techniques relates to and shapes the theme, you will also be demonstrating how the writer 'create[s] meanings and effects.'

Now, in my experience, language analysis is the most important element of AO2. You will also notice, however, that AO2 asks students to comment on 'form and structure.' Again, the thematic approach has your back – because though simply shoehorning in a point on form or structure will feel jarring, when you bring these points up while discussing a theme, as a means to further a thematic argument, you will again organically be discussing the way it 'create[s] meanings and effects.'

(As an aside, there is often confusion when it comes to the terms 'structure' and 'form'. Generally speaking, 'form' relates to patterns and arrangements an author has chosen: is the poem in sonnet form? has the author opted to arrange the content as a dramatic monologue? how many lines and stanzas has the author used? 'Structure', on the other hand, is more to do with the positioning of rhymes, literary techniques, or metrical anomalies, and the impact this has on the reader. However, there is debate over these terms in academic circles, and they can certainly be construed as overlapping in various ways. At any rate, you want to discuss structure or form at least once in every essay).

The next Assessment Objective you need to be aware of is AO3, which requires students to 'show understanding of the relationships between texts and the contexts in which they were written'. The good news is that comments on context are easy enough to weave into a thematic argument; indeed, the theme gives the student a chance to bring up context in a relevant and fitting way. After all, you don't want it to look like you've just shoehorned a contextual factoid into the mix. (Also, keep in mind that this particular Assessment Objective is *only relevant to responses to the anthology* – it is *not* in play when dealing with Unseen Poetry).

Finally, you have AO4 – known also as "spelling and grammar." Truth be told, this guide is not geared towards AO4. My advice? Make sure you are reading plenty of books and articles, because the more you read, the better your spelling and grammar will be. Also, before the exam, perhaps make a list of words you struggle to spell but often find yourself using in essays, and commit them to memory.

Final comment

My hope is that this book, by demonstrating how to select relevant themes, will help you feel more confident in doing so yourself. I believe it is also worth mentioning that the themes Anthony has picked out are by no means definitive. Asked the very same question, someone else may pick out different themes, and write an answer that is just as good (if not better!). Obviously the exam is not likely to be fun – my memory of them is pretty much the exact opposite. But still, this is one of the very few chances that you will get at GCSE level to actually be creative. And to my mind at least, that was always more enjoyable – if enjoyable is the right word – than simply demonstrating that I had memorised loads of facts.

You'd be surprised how cheaply you can get hold of poetry these days!

INTRODUCTION

One of the biggest points I try to make with my students is that all examinations are a chance to show off. Unfortunately, with the return of linear exams a few years ago, students now only really get one shot at proving their knowledge in their exam. In the context of the poetry anthology, that's two (relatively short) essays to let your examiner know just how much you know.

It's key, then, that your answers are full of detail. This has a practical benefit, as a detailed knowledge of the text is also a way of gaining AO1 marks, but there are ways it can be used to get marks elsewhere. For example, spend time understanding the details behind each poem: some poems from the anthology were written with someone specific in mind (Byron's 'She Walks in Beauty' or Dove's 'Cozy Apologia', for example), whilst others were written during the same historical moment (Keats, Shelley, Wordsworth and Byron were all famous poets from the Romantic period). Taking the time to understand the anthology **as a whole and the connections between poems** in this way can really help.

On the point about showing off your knowledge, remember that **brackets are your friends**. Brackets can be used to include extra information. When writing English literature essays, they can be a really good way of making it clear where or what in the poem you're referring to. You can put a quotation in brackets just to back up your point, or you might want to include an additional thought or detail alongside your other points. There are plenty of examples of both throughout these essay plans.

However, don't forget that it should be extraneous information only that goes in brackets (meaning information that's a helpful bonus or just an additional thought) – anything that is essential should be in the sentence properly. But when you've got brackets with extra information, it subtly stresses to the examiner **how much** knowledge you've got at your fingertips. You might see how I also use brackets to draw attention to specific quotations if I'm discussing a larger quotation – this focus makes it clearer for your examiner to understand the point you're making.

The Wordsworthian equivalent of a selfie! An extract from Wordsworth's poem, The Prelude, features in the anthology.

Which leads me onto my next point – **take the time to study the poems in detail**. You can't take the anthology in with you, but students who know all of their English Literature texts in detail do better. In part, it's because AO1 is looking to assess how well you know the texts (what the mark scheme calls having a 'perceptive understanding of the text'), but there's also an element of just being adequately prepared. Students who have revised in detail have done the mental gymnastics already – they've thought about the poems, have prepared potential connections and have even planned out essays. Your examiner doesn't know you – the only evidence they've got of how hard you've worked throughout the two years studying for your GCSE exams is the completed answer paper in front of them, so make sure you've shown them just how hard you've worked therein.

One of the simplest ways you can signal to your examiner that you're analysing a text (also known as creating meaning, so AO2) is using **signposting** language. Your school might call it something different, but when you use words like 'highlights', 'emphasises', 'amplifies', 'illustrates' and 'reflects' (there are others) you're letting your examiner know you're about to talk about the **effect** of a specific technique. So much of good exam technique is having a **clear written style** and signposting is a key way to achieve this – you'll see throughout the plans below how I always use these words **after** I've named the technique and given the evidence (often quotations) before exploring what these techniques do. I'm basically attaching a sign saying 'Here's the right sort of stuff you're looking for, give me marks'.

Blake's original artwork that accompanied his poem, 'London', in an 1826 collection. Guide your examiner — just like this!

A consistent theme in the Examiner's Reports (which are **always** worth reading across all of your subjects – they tell you what good and bad answers look like, and you shouldn't underestimate the importance of the latter) is that some students seem not to know the poems that well, and therefore have to treat the first anthology poem essay like an unseen response. Why this is problematic should be obvious. You wouldn't just arrive at the London Marathon ready to run without training, so why treat your GCSE work in the same way? Preparation is key to success, and whilst it takes time, you should see any time spent in the build-up to your exams revising as an investment in your future life. 'Future You' will thank 'Past You' on results day.

Also, a quick note on context. This is an English Literature exam, *not* a History exam. The exam board don't want paragraphs outlining the influence of the Bosnian conflict on Armitage's 'The Manhunt', nor do they need reams of writing on Wordsworth's love of ice-skating (although, who knew?!). But remember that context is key – AO3 is an essential objective, and so aim to include context in every paragraph.

The key to good context use in English Literature is to show how the context is reflected in the text. One simple way of showing this is ensuring that you always follow some contextual information with textual analysis. Never just throw it on the end of a paragraph – your examiner will know it's an afterthought, and it's not that engaging. A good revision activity can be attaching certain contextual points to certain analytical points for each poem – that way, you know you're covering the context and it lets you practice that vital hitching that will get you the higher marks.

Finally, a note on reading. As with any form of study, reading widely in an area can help, and poetry is no different.

However, you might then ask: "Where do I start?" Well, simply, start where you're interested.

As part of this course, you've studied a wide-ranging and interesting anthology, and some of the central themes – love, war, nature and time – are easily accessible. To help you find some other age-appropriate poetry, you might want to consider looking at poetry anthologies from different exam boards that are actually clustered around central themes: if you've enjoyed Duffy's 'Valentine', try AQA's 'Love and Relationships' anthology; if Blake's 'London' has you thinking about how cities are presented in literature, try Edexcel's 'Time and Place' anthology; or if Owen's 'Dulce et Decorum Est' has you interested in war poetry elsewhere and by others, try AQA's 'Power and Conflict' or OCR's 'Conflict' anthologies. Equally, you could explore other themes – try OCR's 'Youth and Age' anthology or maybe Edexcel's 'Belonging' anthology.

A drawing of Esthwaite Water, the lake on which William Wordsworth learnt to skate.

The more poetry you read, the more you'll be able to appreciate. It's a simple and easy way to help you prepare for your GCSE work, **especially** the unseen poetry section. Plus, there are so many resources online now, it's a lot easier to read **and understand** a poem – if at first it's not clear, try reading it again; if you're still struggling, pop the poem into a search engine followed by the words "outline", "explanation" or "analysis". There'll be a resource that will explain the work to you. Remember, be patient and give yourself time to sit down properly and read – you wouldn't leave a cinema five minutes into a movie because you don't understand it or because it hasn't grabbed your attention, so why would you give up on what you're reading because it didn't "grab" you in the opening lines?

All of this applies to the other two "types" of literature you explore at GCSE level: novels and plays. Allow yourself some relaxation time to read widely. The point is to just read – be inquisitive and led by what interests you. It feels like there's always this pressure to study "the classics" like William Shakespeare, Williams Wordsworth, Jane Austen or Charles Dickens, but it won't have an impact if you don't **enjoy it.** I always say to my students and their parents, "I don't care what you read, as long as you're reading." But the more you read, the more you flex your imaginative muscles – to continue the comparison, muscles need training to become strong, just like the imagination. If you devote the time now, you'll see results (speaking of which, I should probably go to the gym more).

I'll get off my soap box now, but it cannot be stressed enough that students who read independently often achieve higher grades in **both** their English Literature and English Language exams, as it helps immeasurably with the creative writing elements in the latter course. **Reading should be a habit or hobby**, not a task or chore, so grab your favourite drink (mine's a cup of tea), sit down in a comfy chair and read something, anything – you'll thank me later when you find the entirety of your English work getting easier.

Rita Dove, one of the poets in your anthology, receiving the 2011 National Medal of Arts from then US President, Barack Obama. Goes to show that poetry really can take you places!

THE POETRY ANTHOLOGY

PAIRING I: WAR
'DULCE ET DECORUM EST' & 'THE MANHUNT'

Guidance

For the Part 1 question, it's always good to track through the poem. This means to cover it in its entirety, working through it step by step. You'll notice that my first paragraph will often begin with the first line of the poem – starting confidently with your analysis as you begin shows the examiner that you're completely in control of the material. It also gives you an easy way of starting a paragraph – there's no need to come up with some pithy statement, just jump straight in.

As you'll see elsewhere, a similar logic applies to writing about the end of a poem at the end of your answer; conclusions are difficult, so writing about the end of a text often brings your answer to a natural close whilst also allowing you slip in that final bit of analysis or a reflection on the poem's theme (see my later tips for concluding your essays throughout the book). You want to leave as good an impression on the examiner's mind as possible so that they're thinking about you and your work positively as they decide what mark to give you, and this simple way of beginning and ending your work offers a nice level of clarity that should not be under-estimated.

Part a: Read Wilfred Owen's 'Dulce Et Decorum Est'. Owen's poem is about war. How does Owen present war in the poem? Remember to refer to the contexts of the poem in your answer. [15 marks]

Dulce Et Decorum Est
By Wilfred Owen

Bent double, like old beggars under sacks,
Knock-kneed, coughing like hags, we cursed through
    sludge,
Till on the haunting flares we turned our backs,
And towards our distant rest began to trudge.
Men marched asleep. Many had lost their boots,
But limped on, blood-shod. All went lame; all blind;
Drunk with fatigue; deaf even to the hoots
Of gas-shells dropping softly behind.

Gas! GAS! Quick, boys!—An ecstasy of fumbling
Fitting the clumsy helmets just in time,
But someone still was yelling out and stumbling
And flound'ring like a man in fire or lime.—
Dim through the misty panes and thick green light,
As under a green sea, I saw him drowning.

In all my dreams before my helpless sight,

He plunges at me, guttering, choking, drowning.

If in some smothering dreams, you too could pace
Behind the wagon that we flung him in,
And watch the white eyes writhing in his face,
His hanging face, like a devil's sick of sin;
If you could hear, at every jolt, the blood
Come gargling from the froth-corrupted lungs,
Obscene as cancer, bitter as the cud
Of vile, incurable sores on innocent tongues,—
My friend, you would not tell with such high zest
To children ardent for some desperate glory,
The old Lie: *Dulce et decorum est
Pro patria mori.*

Introduction

Throughout the book, I'm going to show you various ways of opening and closing your essays. However, the idea behind the introduction will be the same: have a simple summary of the poem that refers to the question topic. This way, you're making it clear to the examiner that you understand the poem(s) you're analysing and that you're in control of the material. Keep your introductions simple – you want to have more time for a final flourish in your conclusion, as that's the last thing your examiner will read before they decide your mark.

> "Wilfred Owen's 'Dulce et Decorum Est' explores not the grandeur of war but its horrors; it explores the abysmal trench conditions and how the soldiers who fight in these battles are left to struggle both during and after their time fighting."

Theme/Paragraph One: Owen's poem challenged the expectations around the genre of war poetry, in part by focusing on the soldier's suffering.

- Some of the most famous war poems, from Homer's The Iliad through to Tennyson's 'Charge of the Light Brigade', focus on ideas of glory and patriotism. They in part ignore the constant tension that living in a warzone can bring. From the beginning of the poem, however, Owen makes clear how challenging the trench conditions were during World War One. The soldiers are described as being 'Bent double, like old beggars under sacks'. This simile[1] presents the soldiers as weak and desperate, a marked contrast to what might be expected from war poetry. [*AO1 for incorporating a textual reference to justify and support an interpretation. AO2 for close analysis of the author's language.*]
- This challenging of the reader's expectations is continued in the second simile in the second line – the soldiers are described as 'coughing like hags' – thereby presenting an intense image of suffering, with the image of 'hags' carrying connotations[2] of feebleness and having a withered[3] quality. [*AO2 for close analysis of the author's language.*]
- The first stanza of Owen's poem cumulatively[4] builds on the soldier's suffering. The suggestion of the 'haunting flares' creates an almost nightmarish setting, which is further amplified[5] by the heavy rhyme of 'sludge' and 'trudge'; the repetition of 'all' in 'All went lame; all blind' captures the widespread suffering

being faced, and the metaphor 'Drunk with fatigue' illustrates how dazed and out of control these men are. Owen's tone at the beginning of the poem, then, is one of pity – these are not celebrated soldiers but tired men who have been defeated by the conditions of the war in which they are fighting. [*AO2 for close analysis of the author's use of form and language*].

Theme/Paragraph Two: As the poem continues, Owen vividly[6] portrays an attack on the trenches and directly addresses the present to suggest how damaging war is.

- In the second stanza, Owen depicts a gas attack on the trenches. Lime gas, with its distinctive green colour, was a common chemical used during World War One, although the war's unprecedented death toll was also the result of more destructive machinery. Owen's repeated use of sea motifs[7] in the second stanza ('flound'ring like a man in fire or lime' and 'I saw him drowning') adds an overwhelming sense of desperation to the poem, which is then directly explored in the third stanza. This short couplet graphically[8] records how this dying man haunts the soldier ('In all my dreams'), with the list of verbs ('guttering, choking, drowning') adding a particularly visceral[9] and uncomfortable tone, which is amplified by the condensed, unrhymed couplet. Furthermore, that Owen returns to the word 'drowning', again at the end of the stanza, creates a tone of inevitability – the horror of war cannot be escaped. [*AO1 for incorporating textual references to justify and support an interpretation. AO2 for close analysis of the author's use of form and language. AO3 for demonstrating an understanding of how the context shapes the text*].

- Of course, there was little dignity in the trenches, with the wet conditions matched in their discomfort by the constant sound of artillery fire and anticipation of going over the top. The soldier's death in Owen's poem is continually presented as unpleasant and uncomfortable, with the verb 'flung' in the fourth stanza indicative of how little dignity there is for the dead soldier. The alliterative 'watch the white eyes writhing in his face' amplifies the connotations of pain that come with the word 'writhing'. [*AO2 for close analysis of the author's language. AO3 for demonstrating an understanding of how the context shapes the text*].
- All of which culminates[10] when Owen directly addresses the reader ('If you could hear'). At this moment, however, instead of diluting[11] his message, Owen vividly returns to the dead soldier's 'froth-corrupted lungs', which are described as 'Obscene as cancer, bitter as the cud'. This pair of similes, intensely placed on the same line, use a language of illness and disgust to highlight once again how unforgiving war is. [*AO2 for close analysis of the author's use of structure and language*].

Conclusion

You might notice that my conclusions for the Part 1 questions often end with an extra piece of analysis, usually some language analysis. It's important to try to always add just that little bit extra in, especially as you haven't got that long to write the Part 1 answer. Giving that final piece of analysis just helps to show your examiner that you're in complete control of the material. Don't feel like a conclusion has to be repetitive: you should be adding that finishing touch to show the examiner how knowledgeable you are about the material.

"Owen's poetry unapologetically presents what it's like to live through and fight in a war. The apostrophe[12] 'My friend' at the poem's end adds a tone is that is both intimate and antagonistic – he wants readers to know the truth and to stop believing 'The old Lie' that in war there is 'desperate glory'. Instead, it seems, it's all death and violence."

A portrait of Wilfred Owen, taken from a 1920 edition of his poems.

Part b: Choose one other poem from the anthology in which the poet also writes about war. Compare the way the poet presents war in your chosen poem with the way Wilfred Owen presents war in 'Dulce Et Decorum Est'. [25 marks]

In your answer you should compare:

• **the content and structure of the poems – what they are about and how they are organised**

• **how the writers create effects, using appropriate terminology where relevant**

• **the contexts of the poems, and how these may have influenced the ideas in them.**

Introduction

Generally I'd advise you to keep your introductions short and simple. State your partner poem and explore briefly how it works with your first poem, and then move on. But sometimes you might want to get a little bit of analysis in, and I do just that below (but try to keep this just for the **beginnings** of the poems – anything else should be saved, really, for the body of the essay).

Also, don't forget that **you can repeat the same analysis from your Part a answer in your Part b response** (a point that's been made across numerous Examiner's Reports), but I'd advise you to at least change the wording a bit so that it doesn't look quite so familiar (you'll see I comment on trench conditions again in the first section, but phrase it differently and add slightly different details).

> "Alongside Owen's 'Dulce et Decorum Est', Simon Armitage's 'The Manhunt' presents war as utterly destructive. Together these poems are suitably angry at how war can leave soldiers fragile and broken, with the damage leaving a legacy of suffering. It is appropriate, then, that Armitage's 'The Manhunt' begins as might be expected from a love poem ('After the first phase, / after passionate nights and intimate days') – war is not something that is easily left behind and it leaves its mark on all who fight in it."

Theme/Paragraph One: In both poems there is a tone of anger towards war and how it transforms the people who go out to fight for what they believe in.

- At the opening of 'Dulce et Decorum Est', Owen starts with an unexpected image: instead of the celebratory tone that might be expected from war poetry, he presents the soldiers as weak and desperate. The simile 'like old beggars under sacks' highlights the poverty and feebleness of the soldiers,[13] whilst the numerous caesuras during these opening lines slow the poem's pace, forcing the reader to pause and linger on this image. [*AO1 for incorporating textual references to justify and support an interpretation.*

AO2 for close analysis of the author's use of form and language].
- Owen draws particular attention to the terrible trench conditions in World War One. Trenches were wet, muddy and uncomfortable; diseases like dysentery and cholera were common and the soldiers had to contend with the harsh weather. It is little surprise, then, that Owen states 'All went lame; all blind; / Drunk with fatigue'. Owen pointedly uses 'All' to illustrate how widespread this suffering was, whilst the metaphor 'Drunk with fatigue' carries connotations of being out of control and dazed. These soldiers 'cursed through sludge' and the opening stanza consistently stresses the incessant[14] suffering these soldiers face. Even attempting to reach the 'distant rest' of death requires the men to 'trudge', with the rhyme of 'trudge' and 'sludge' adding a tone of heavy difficulty to this activity.[15] Owen is therefore very critical of the trench conditions and through this there is a tone of anger at how the soldiers are left to fight against seemingly insurmountable[16] conditions. [*AO2 for close analysis of the author's use of form and language. AO3 for demonstrating an understanding of how the context shapes the text*].
- <u>Pivot to comparison:</u> Where Owen captures the experiences of those soldiers fighting in the trenches, Armitage's 'The Manhunt' explores what happens with the soldiers return home. In the second couplet, it describes how a 'frozen river [...] ran through his face' – Armitage's metaphor highlights not only the pain and discomfort felt by these soldiers but it also illustrates how shocking and grievous the damage is. This is seen again in the third couplet, where the

'blown hinge of his lower jaw' is described, which stresses the damage these soldiers must face – the focus on the body throughout the poem highlights how this is a journey through pain, and therefore there is a notable tone of anger and frustration at how these men have just been left to suffer. [*AO2 for close analysis of the author's use of language*].

Theme/Paragraph Two: Both poems suggest the fragility of the soldiers who fight in the war.

- Armitage's poem is set within a domestic[17] frame – it is written from the wife's perspective of her husband's return and the physical and emotional suffering they both experience. The poem emerged from the documentary Forgotten Heroes: The Not Dead and was read by Laura Bridges. It is a reminder of the PTSD that many soldiers go through. Hence it is unsurprising that Armitage uses a language of fragility. For example, in the fourth couplet[18] it is noticed how the soldier has a 'porcelain collar-bone', which carries connotations of frailty, whilst in the fifth couplet it is described how the soldier has a 'fractured rudder[19] of shoulder-blade', which implies the soldier now needs some guidance. [*AO2 for close analysis of the author's use of language. AO3 for demonstrating an understanding of how the context shapes the text*].
- These metaphors[20] cumulatively create an image of the human body that is barely held together. The anaphora[21] of 'only then' and 'and' at the beginning of the first six stanzas, which are all connected by enjambment,[22] gives the suggestion that 'The Manhunt' is a list of how the soldier's body has broken

down. Like Dr Frankenstein, the wife is left to pull together these now disparate[23] (and damaged) parts of the human body. 'Only then', it is noted in stanza seven, 'could I bind the struts / and climb the rungs of his broken ribs' – Armitage's metaphors suggest how those are attempts to heal the soldier but it is a perilous[24] and difficult process. [*AO1 for incorporating textual references to justify and support an interpretation. AO2 for close analysis of the author's use of form and language*].

- Pivot to comparison: Owen is also concerned with how damaged and fragile those who fight in war become. After stanza two, in which a gas attack is depicted in graphic detail, Owen describes how the image of the 'drowning' man haunts the poem's narrator even after he has left the trenches. It is described how 'In all my dreams, before my helpless sight, / He plunges at me, guttering, choking, drowning.' Against the longer stanzas, this detached couplet creates an inconsistent, almost deformed, poem. At home, the soldier is constantly reminded of what he saw on the front line, with the verbs 'plunges' and 'choking' emphasising the violent desperation of the dying soldier. There is also little dignity for these soldiers – it is described in the fourth stanza how the dead are 'flung' into a wagon – and Owen therefore illustrates how fragile these men are. [*AO1 for incorporating textual references to justify and support an interpretation. AO2 for close analysis of the author's use of structure and language*].

Theme/Paragraph Three: Together, the poems explore the legacy of war, with both focusing in

different ways on those who are left at home.

- The title of Armitage's poem, 'The Manhunt', highlights how something has been lost and must be found. Moreover, in the shortest couplet the speaker describes how she could 'feel the hurt / of his grazed heart' – the adjective 'grazed' has two connotations, as it notes how the damage is both slight and permanent. Furthermore, there is a contrasting language in describing the bullet as a 'foetus of metal' – Armitage's metaphor juxtaposes the caring and delicate suggestion of a 'foetus' with the harsh reality of the bullet. [*AO1 for incorporating textual references to justify and support an interpretation. AO2 for close analysis of the author's use of language*].
- Although inspired by a soldier's experiences in the Bosnian war, 'The Manhunt' explores the effects of war on an individual more broadly. PTSD can affect any soldier, and this poem reads more generally like an account of what happens to soldiers when they come home. This focus on the damage sustained by the soldier continues towards the end of the poem, which describes the 'unexploded mine / buried deep in his mind'. Armitage's metaphor illustrates a sense of danger and instability that contextualises the earlier images of fragility – everything might be destroyed at any moment. [*AO2 for close analysis of the author's use of language. AO3 for demonstrating an understanding of how the context shapes the text*].
- <u>Pivot to comparison:</u> Owen wrote 'Dulce et Decorum Est' whilst recuperating in Craiglockhart in October 1917. At this point, the patriotic impulse that had drawn many soldiers to war was dissipating as

accounts of the trench conditions made their way back to the families waiting for news about their loved ones. At the beginning of the fourth stanza,[25] Owen moves towards the reader, presuming they are sat in the comfort of their home whilst soldiers die. The direct apostrophe 'My friend' adds a forced friendliness to the poem, which is then matched by the writer's frustration as they reiterate the 'old Lie' of 'Dulce et decorum est / Pro patria mori'.[26] The grand, noble Latin is contrasted with the graphic imagery of the poem and the apparent hypocrisy of those who used this line to convince young men to sign up for war. These young men are referred to as 'children', which illustrates their naivety at going off to fight.

[*AO1 for incorporating textual references to justify and support an interpretation. AO2 for close analysis of the author's use of language. AO3 for demonstrating an understanding of how the context shapes the text*].

Conclusion

Try to never begin your conclusion with 'In conclusion' – just imagine how many answers your examiner is going to read where that phrase is used. It's formulaic (meaning it follows a set formula) and a bit boring. The language you use should suitably indicate that you're bringing your essay to a close. In the Introduction to this section, I stated the importance of signposting language for analysis; signposting language can also be used to note comparisons, evaluation and, importantly, conclusions. Use words like 'therefore' and 'overall' at the ends of your paragraphs and in your conclusion, to let your examiner know you're moving into the final section of your work (and don't have over-long conclusions, either).

In this conclusion, I'm bringing in a third poem from the anthology. This way, I'm showing my expanded knowledge of the anthology. It also makes having 'something fresh' to say a bit easier, but make sure you link it to the broader ideas explored in your essay, otherwise it might feel irrelevant or unfocused.

> "Both poems therefore present war as unglamorous. Compared with a poem like Brooke's 'The Soldier', which focuses more on the patriotic glory that comes with fighting for your country, these poems do not celebrate war but merely highlight its brutality and lasting damage. Together, they are enduring reminders of the sacrifices others have made for our daily freedoms."

Simon Armitage wrote 'The Manhunt' for the documentary film Forgotten Heroes: The Not Dead. Photo copyright © Alexander Williamson.

PAIRING II: DEATH
'A WIFE IN LONDON' & 'MAMETZ WOOD'

Part a: Read Thomas Hardy's 'A Wife in London'. Hardy's poem is about death. How does Hardy present death in the poem? Remember to refer to the contexts of the poem in your answer. [15 marks]

A Wife in London
By Thomas Hardy

I--The Tragedy

She sits in the tawny vapour
   That the City lanes have uprolled,
   Behind whose webby fold on fold
Like a waning taper
   The street-lamp glimmers cold.

A messenger's knock cracks smartly,
   Flashed news is in her hand
   Of meaning it dazes to understand
Though shaped so shortly:
   He--has fallen--in the far South Land ...

II--The Irony

'Tis the morrow; the fog hangs thicker,
   The postman nears and goes:
   A letter is brought whose lines disclose
By the firelight flicker
   His hand, whom the worm now knows:

Fresh--firm--penned in highest feather -
   Page-full of his hoped return,
   And of home-planned jaunts by brake and burn
In the summer weather,
   And of new love that they would learn.

Introduction

One of the ways you might want to introduce your essays is to use some contextual information. This can be a good way to ensure you're getting those context marks from the opening lines, but as always with context don't go into too much detail – save that for the body of the essay. Hopefully you can see below how I've used contextual information but only in a light way, and at the end of the introduction I refer to the poem that's being discussed.

"Hardy's 'A Wife in London' is about the effects of war, with a soldier's wife receiving the news by telegram[1] that her husband will not return. Although the poem might refer to the Boer war, Hardy depicts a scene that is generic for any soldier and their family, showing readers how quietly devastating death can be.[2]"

Theme/Paragraph One: Hardy's poem heightens the atmosphere of loss in 'The Tragedy', the first section, through the detailed description of the setting.

- From the opening lines of 'A Wife in London', Hardy creates a dark atmosphere of loss. Given Hardy's ability as a novelist, it should be unsurprising that he creates such a vivid and evocative[3] setting within the opening stanza of the poem, especially Victorian London, which was dirty, impoverished, and full of sadness and difficulty. London is described through a lens of gloom and darkness: there is a 'tawny[4] vapour' hanging over the city and 'The street-lamp glimmers cold.' Throughout the city, light is being overcome by the darkness, foreshadowing the wife's approaching news of her loss: the fog's effect on light is described as 'like a waning taper', with Hardy's simile emphasising the increasing weakness of the light. The fog itself is also presented like a spider, creating a 'webby fold on fold' around its environment – this language of entrapment creates a sense of anxiety and foreboding[5] to the poem. [*AO1 for incorporating textual references* to justify and support an interpretation. AO2 for close analysis of the author's use of language. AO3 for demonstrating an understanding of how the context shapes the text].

- Moreover, 'A Wife in London' is written in the present tense, which adds an immediacy to the work that makes it impossible to ignore the impact of the soldier's death. Thus in the second stanza when 'A messenger's knock cracks smartly' to deliver the telegram, it is surprising, with the word 'cracks' adding a particularly destructive note to the development. Hardy also creates a sense of detachment to the poem by writing it in the third person ('She sits') – together, the present tense and third person combine to give the impression that the same event is happening across the world, illustrating how damaging war is and how lonely the wife now is and will be in the future. [AO2 for close analysis of the author's use of language].

- 'A Wife in London' captures a moment in history where telegrams were used to report a soldier's death. They were quicker than letters, which leads to the situation in the poem where the wife receives notice of her husband's death before his letter. Having established such a dreary atmosphere, the euphemism[6] 'He – has fallen – in the far South Land...' carries an immense emotional weight. Hardy's use of dashes and ellipses[7] highlights the wife's grief, as if she cannot process the new normal – her world has become broken, just like the sentence structure. [AO2 for close analysis of the author's use of form and language. AO3 for demonstrating an understanding of how the context shapes the text].

Theme/Paragraph Two: There's a pervasive[8] sense of irony throughout the poem's second section, which highlights the tragedy of the poem's narrative.

- At the beginning of the poem's second section, 'The Irony', Hardy continues certain motifs from the first section. To begin with, the fog now 'hangs thicker', with Hardy again using pathetic fallacy[9] to imply the personal darkness that the wife is facing having received the news about her husband. Furthermore, the letter from the postman is read by 'the firelight flicker' – like the 'waning taper' before, Hardy here uses the imagery of weakening light to suggest how darkness is increasingly encroaching on the wife's mentality, with the word 'flicker' carrying connotations of weakness. [*AO1 for incorporating textual references to justify and support an interpretation. AO2 for close analysis of the author's use of language*].
- Hardy's anti-war stance can be felt throughout the entire poem. Hardy graphically states 'His hand, whom the worm now knows'. This shocking reference to the soldier's death introduces the irony of the second section, as in the fourth stanza Hardy changes the tone by focusing on the positive imagery and optimism of the soldier's letter. Nonetheless, it's hard to ignore the irony at the opening of the fourth stanza, 'Fresh – firm –', which refers to the tone of the words written by the solider but that is contrasted to his death. He is no longer 'fresh' or 'firm' but dead in 'the far South Land', a reference to South Africa, the site

of the Boer War. [*AO2 for close analysis of the author's use of language. AO3 for demonstrating an understanding of how the context shapes the text*].

- The optimism in the soldier's letters heightens the tragedy of his death. He writes about the simple pleasures he looks forward to, getting out of the glum city and moving towards a rural idyll ('home-planned jaunts by brake and burn'). These wishes were 'penned in the highest feather' – Hardy's metaphor adds an element of lightness and simplicity, capturing the soldier's hopefulness at the point of writing. The tone of hope in the letter is thus cruelly deflated by the soldier's death, amplifying the tone of loss that permeates the poem. [*AO2 for close analysis of the author's use of language*].

Conclusion

"Hardy's 'A Wife in London' shows how quiet and unexpected death can be. It is a poem on a universal theme – the death of a loved one fighting abroad. It reminds readers that with death comes the end of not just one life but the life that would be shared with another: 'of new love that they would learn.' It is in this missed opportunity that the tragedy of Hardy's poem is felt at its fullest and most powerful."

Part b: Choose one other poem from the anthology in which the poet also writes about death. Compare the way the poet presents death in your chosen poem with the way Thomas Hardy presents death in 'A Wife in London'. [25 marks]

In your answer you should compare:

• **the content and structure of the poems – what they are about and how they are organised**

• **how the writers create effects, using appropriate terminology where relevant**

• **the contexts of the poems, and how these may have influenced the ideas in them.**

Introduction

When comparing poems, you might want to use the relevant historical context to structure your comparison. Indeed, it's difficult when writing about war poetry to **not** include plenty of context; the challenge, however, is sifting through and being selective in the material you present. Below I discuss Owen Sheers's 'Mametz Wood', but note how I don't go into excessive detail about the before and after of the battle – I try to keep strictly to the relevant facts and use that as part of my analysis.

Don't ever just stick a quotation in your paragraphs. Always have a little tag that mentions the poet's name and where the quotation is from. That way, it feels like you're in control of the material. Furthermore, make sure you stay focused on the question set. You'll notice in my answer below I'm often having to balance my answer, which uses two war poems, with a focus on death. It would be easy here to slip into writing an essay about the effects of war in both poems – you need to always make sure you explicitly make your answer **relevant** to the question and specific topic that's been set, otherwise your examiner might not make the connection and assess your work as lacking focus.

> "Hardy's 'A Wife in London' makes for an interesting pairing with Owen Sheers's 'Mametz Wood', especially on the theme of death.[10] Both poems confront the reality of war, but neither poem is about the experiences of young men on the front line. Instead, the poems suggest the impact of war on the lives and communities of those at home. Together, they suggest the fragility of human life and happiness and the anger that many feel when people give their lives in service for their country."

Theme/Paragraph One: Hardy's poem depicts how death can be devastating for a personal relationship, but Sheers focuses more on the continuing impact death and war has on the community.

- The title of Hardy's poem suggests that this is a generic scene – 'A Wife in London' is left alone to suffer. Similarly, in being written in the third person ('She sits') there is an air of detachment to the poem –

it is as if Hardy is observing an occurrence in London that is as common as the poverty and deprivation that was so prevalent during his life. Similarly, the poem is written in the present tense, which gives the narrative an immediacy – as readers, we watch as the messenger arrives and flinch as his 'knock cracks smartly', with the verb and adverb together registering how sharp the movement is whilst the 'flashed news' highlights how quickly it is delivered to her. Through these features, Hardy creates a universal poem that feels intensely personal. [*AO1 for incorporating textual references to justify and support an interpretation. AO2 for close analysis of the author's use of language*].

- In 'A Wife in London', Hardy uses a repeated motif of light being overcome by darkness to symbolise the soldier's death and the anguish that his wife is now going through. In the first stanza, a streetlamp's light is described 'Like a waning taper', with Hardy's simile emphasising how symbolically the wife's hope at her husband's return is about to be extinguished. Similarly, the streetlamp 'glimmers cold', suggesting how it offers no warmth or comfort anymore. This language of darkness is continued in the poem's second section, where it is described how the husband's letter is read 'By the firelight flicker', with the verb 'flicker' carrying connotations of weakness. Hardy's language therefore heightens the atmosphere of loss, representing the darkness that comes with losing a loved one. [*AO2 for close analysis of the author's use of language.*]

- <u>Pivot to comparison:</u> Where Hardy shows how death can affect a loved one, Sheers emphasises how death and war has a lasting impact on both communities and the land. 'Mametz Wood' begins 'For years afterwards the farmers found them', which illustrates how the horrors of war are experienced not just by soldiers on the battlefield, but also by those who live near these sites of carnage for many years after the war. Sheers's poem reminds readers that following the unprecedented levels of death and destruction of World War One, it was not always possible to send bodies home to be buried; instead, they had to be buried quickly, often unidentified. When Sheers terms the bodies 'the wasted young', he draws on two meanings: firstly, the word 'wasted' refers to the decaying bodies, but secondly it also refers to the wasted lives of these young men. Sheers's poem wants to recognise the sacrifice of the 38th Welsh Division who died during the battle of Mametz Wood, hence this elegiac[11] poem becomes a memorial to them and their actions, gesturing to how their deaths have had a lasting impact on the world around them. [*AO1 for incorporating textual references to justify and support an interpretation. AO2 for close analysis of the author's use of language. AO3 for demonstrating an understanding of how the context shapes the text*].

Theme/Paragraph Two: Both poems stress how fragile humans are, with the deaths of the soldiers presented as a tragedy for everyone whose lives come into contact with them.

- Hardy uses the setting of the poem to create a tone of darkness and tragedy that powerfully foreshadows[12] the soldier's death. The wife is alone in a dark city, sitting in a 'tawny vapour', which creates an image of London covered in a thick and yellow fog. Due to the pollution that came in part as a result of the Industrial Revolution, these heavy fogs were common in the city; Hardy describes the 'webby fold on fold' it has over the inhabitants, which carries connotations of entrapment and anxiety: the fog, like a spider, has trapped all of the inhabitants, with the sense of loss and dread they feel at the soldier's death now being inevitable. When the telegram comes, when 'Flashed news is in her hand', it is 'shaped so shortly: / He – has fallen – in the far South Land...' Alongside the euphemism ('has fallen'), Hardy uses dashes and ellipses to break the flow of line, emphasising the wife's grief. [*AO1 for incorporating textual references to justify and support an interpretation. AO2 for close analysis of the author's use of form and language*].

- Pivot to comparison: Sheers presents the brutality of war and the fragility of the soldiers more directly than Hardy does. In the second stanza, Sheers describes some of the skeletal pieces found in the grave: 'the china plate of a shoulder blade, / the relic of a finger, the blown / and broken bird's egg of a skull'. Sheers's language ('china plate' and 'bird's egg') emphasises the fragility[13] and vulnerability of these soldiers. However, the language simultaneously suggests an admiration for these soldiers, as the reference points also focus on objects that are valuable, with the word 'relic', for example, illustrating how significant and almost sacred these bones are. Sheers's language therefore elevates the soldiers in their death, transforming their skeletons into objects that should

- be respected and valued. [*AO2 for close analysis of the author's use of language*].
- The battle of Mametz Wood in July 1916 was blighted by poor decisions (soldiers were commanded to charge across open fields during broad daylight) and miscommunications, with the Welsh soldiers fighting hand-to-hand with their enemies amidst friendly fire.[14] Sheers's poem emphasises the sacrifice of these men but there is also a tone of frustration that emerges at points. For example, in the third stanza it is described how 'they were told to walk, not run, / towards the wood and its nesting machine guns.' Sheers's parenthesis,[15] encased by caesuras,[16] not only slows the pace but also draws attention specifically to the thoughtless command; moreover, the notion of the 'nesting machine guns' offers a juxtaposition of the suggestion of nature, care and comfort ('nesting') with the destructive power of the weaponry. Yet the poem's third person narrative voice actively adds the experiences of these soldiers to the annals[17] of history, and Sheers often uses enjambment and long sentences to add a reflective and searching tone to the poem. 'Mametz Wood' therefore keenly stresses the sacrifices made by the soldiers during the battle, celebrating their bravery. [*AO2 for close analysis of the author's use of form and language. AO3 for demonstrating an understanding of how the context shapes the text*].

Theme/Paragraph Three: Whilst the poems emphasise fragility, there's also an anger at how war kills young men and degrades human life.

- When thinking about the genre of war poetry, there are expectations of grand, celebratory and patriotic tones that focus on the glory and accomplishments of leaders and their soldiers. Sheers's 'Mametz Wood', however, pushes back against this, showing the harsh reality of war. This is achieved in part by focusing on how the earth and nature are equally disrupted by war. The earth is personified[18] as a 'sentinel', as if it now needs a great protector; moreover, when the earth thinks back to understand 'what happened' it is described 'like a wound working a foreign body to the surface of the skin.' Sheers's simile alone notes how damaging war is, but there's also something unnatural about the idea of a 'foreign body', which further highlights how these men died in a land that was unfamiliar to them. [*AO1 for incorporating textual references to justify and support an interpretation. AO2 for close analysis of the author's use of language*].
- Furthermore, in the fifth stanza Sheers more directly gives an account of the bodies being unearthed ('This morning'). The skeletons are metaphorically described as 'a broken mosaic of bone linked arm in arm', which picks up the language of beauty and fragility discussed previously. However, this line also highlights the solidarity and support these men had for each other. Sheers then describes the grave, with the skeletons wearing 'boots that outlasted them' and with 'their jaws, those that have them, dropped open.' Sheers's parenthesis again highlights the horror of war, with the shocking addition to the sentence focusing on the injuries these men sustained during the fighting. [*AO2 for close analysis of the author's use of form and language*].

- <u>Pivot to comparison:</u> Hardy had known anti-war sentiments and these can be identified throughout the second half of the poem, entitled 'The Irony', in which the soldier's hope as expressed in a letter to his wife is punctured by his death. The letter was 'penned in the highest feather', with Hardy's metaphor suggesting lightness and optimism – it is 'Page-full of his hoped return'. In the letter, the soldier writes of 'home-planned jaunts by brake and burn / In the summer weather'. Significantly, Hardy's soldier imagines a pastoral idyll[19] away from the dark and cramped confines of London; he looks forward to simple pleasures that are far removed from the battlefield. But the tone of the entire fourth and final stanza is ironic, with the structure of Hardy's poem illustrating how utterly destructive war is both for the soldiers and their loved ones: the cold and factual telegram comes first before the warmth and optimism of the letter. Hardy therefore shows the destructive impact of war and how the families at home are affected, with the soldier's death presented as cruel and unfair given how much life he still had to live. [*AO1 for incorporating textual references to justify and support an interpretation. AO2 for close analysis of the author's use of language*].

Conclusion

"Death is often cruel and unfair, especially when inflicted upon younger bodies. Both Hardy and Sheers suggest the depravity[20] of war and note how it is not just the soldiers who suffer from war but also countless relatives and generations. Yet these poems are key to lend the dead a voice, as Sheers implies at the end of the poem: although the soldiers now have 'absent tongues', their 'unearthing' and the poem provides the opportunity to learn about their sacrifice. Death is, at the very least, not the end."

Thomas Hardy, looking appropriately dour.

PAIRING III: LOVE
'SONNET 43' & 'THE SOLDIER'

Part a: Read Elizabeth Barrett Browning's 'Sonnet 43'. Browning's poem is about love. How does Browning present love in the poem? Remember to refer to the contexts of the poem in your answer. [15 marks]

Sonnet 43
By Elizabeth Barrett Browning

How do I love thee? Let me count the ways.
I love thee to the depth and breadth and height
My soul can reach, when feeling out of sight
For the ends of being and ideal grace.
I love thee to the level of every day's
Most quiet need, by sun and candle-light.
I love thee freely, as men strive for right.
I love thee purely, as they turn from praise.

I love thee with the passion put to use
In my old griefs, and with my childhood's faith.
I love thee with a love I seemed to lose
With my lost saints. I love thee with the breath,
Smiles, tears, of all my life; and, if God choose,
I shall but love thee better after death.

INTRODUCTION

Your introductions need not be long – here I'm directly referring to the question's theme with a slight reference to context before diving straight into my paragraphs. It's simple, yet effective.

> "It is hard not to be taken aback by the intensity with which Elizabeth Barrett Browning declares her love in 'Sonnet 43' – although the woman faced much hardship during her life, this poem shows the transformative impact love can have on an individual."

Theme/Paragraph One: Barrett Browning's poem is an intense meditation on how love can transform a person's life.

- Barrett Browning's 'Sonnet 43' opens with a question: 'How do I love thee?' The direct address frames the poem as if she is answering someone. However Barrett Browning then uses hypophora[1] (the first line continues 'Let me count the ways') to highlight the immediacy with which an answer to the opening question comes to mind. From the beginning, then,

Barrett Browning stresses how prepared she is to openly talk about her love, which clearly continues to have a substantial and ongoing influence on her life. [*AO1 for incorporating textual references to justify and support an interpretation*].

- Throughout the poem, Barrett Browning often starts her lines with 'I love thee'. Barrett Browning's use of anaphora cumulatively builds the multitude of ways in which she loves her partner, which moves from grander themes in the sonnet's octave towards a more human focus on the sestet by exploring how she can love during her own lifetime.[2] As each repetition begins, the reader is aware of both the variety and dedication that Barrett Browning uses as she sets forth her own definition. [*AO2 for close analysis of the author's use of structure and language*].
- Barrett Browning went through various personal traumas in her life: her father was over-protective after the death of her brother who drowned at a young age. When she met Robert Browning aged forty, the intensity of her feelings eventually led to her eloping[3] with him in 1846, which in turn meant she was disinherited by her father (he had forbidden his children from marrying). This autobiographical[4] element to the poem truly adds to the idea of how love can offer an individual salvation.[5] At the beginning of the sestet, Barrett Browning observes 'I love thee with the passions put to use / In my old griefs, and with my childhood's faith.' Barrett Browning suggests how her 'passions' have now been put to better use than fuelling her 'old griefs', a nod perhaps to her earlier years and restrictive childhood, whilst the sentiment that she loves him with 'my childhood's faith' carries

connotations not only of innocence but also of constancy and admiration. She will not leave him. [*AO1 for incorporating textual references to justify and support an interpretation. AO3 for demonstrating an understanding of how the context shapes the text*].

Theme/Paragraph Two: Barrett Browning's love is portrayed as something spiritual and virtuous.[6]

- Barrett Browning spent much of her life unwell and was often sick and confined to her bed. It's unsurprising, then, that 'Sonnet 43' almost portrays love as something akin to salvation – it not only helped remove her from her father's household but also gave her a way of thinking about life that celebrated her for herself, not her capabilities. [*AO3 for demonstrating an understanding of how the context shapes the text*].
- Throughout the poem Barrett Browning capitalises certain words (including 'Grace', 'Right' and 'Praise'), meaning that these words come to represent concepts. For example, the word 'Grace' comes to signify something religious, as if approved by God. Her love is virtuous, almost holy, thus transforming it into something beyond normal human, carnal love – that is, into something divine and spiritual. [*AO1 for incorporating textual references to justify and support an interpretation. AO2 for close analysis of the author's use of language*].
- One of the things that is striking about Barrett Browning's love in the poem is how she balances the larger, complex concepts described above with other simple definitions. For example, 'I love thee to the

level of every day's / Most quiet need, by sun and candlelight' stresses her love to be both daily and constant. That her love exists both day and night ('sun and candlelight' respectively) highlights how her love is unending and dedicated – he gives her life and comforts her at her darkest moments. [*AO1 for incorporating textual references to justify and support an interpretation. AO2 for close analysis of the author's use of language*].

Conclusion

You can also add some contextual information to your conclusions. As always, keep it brief and make sure it's linked directly to the text.

> "Barrett Browning's 'Sonnet 43' was published in *Sonnets from the Portuguese,* a collection of 44 sonnets. In these sonnets, Barrett Browning often declared feelings of desire, longing and attachment. The intimacy with which Barrett Browning addresses her love in 'Sonnet 43' is surprising perhaps for a Victorian woman, and yet the intensity of her emotions and the variety of ways with which she loved Robert Browning continue to be clear over a hundred years after the poem was written. Love is, as the end of the poem suggests, timeless."

A portrait of Elizabeth Barrett Browning.

Part b: Choose one other poem from the anthology in which the poet also writes about love. Compare the way the poet presents love in your chosen poem with the way Elizabeth Barrett Browning presents love in 'Sonnet 43'. [25 marks]

In your answer you should compare:

• **the content and structure of the poems – what they are about and how they are organised**

• **how the writers create effects, using appropriate terminology where relevant**

• **the contexts of the poems, and how these may have influenced the ideas in them.**

The Soldier
By Rupert Brooke

If I should die, think only this of me:
   That there's some corner of a foreign field
That is for ever England. There shall be
   In that rich earth a richer dust concealed;
A dust whom England bore, shaped, made aware,
   Gave, once, her flowers to love, her ways to roam;
A body of England's, breathing English air,
   Washed by the rivers, blest by suns of home.

And think, this heart, all evil shed away,

> A pulse in the eternal mind, no less
>   Gives somewhere back the thoughts by England given;
> Her sights and sounds; dreams happy as her day;
>   And laughter, learnt of friends; and gentleness,
>   In hearts at peace, under an English heaven.

Introduction

Don't be afraid to try something different and have unusual pairings. But if you're making an unexpected pairing, be as direct about it in your introduction as I am below. Remember that in an exam there's little room for subtlety: you want to make it clear to your examiner when you're being a little bit smart.

However, these pairings need to be fruitful and, ultimately, they **need to work**. Examiner's reports have stressed that weaker answers can come from poor partner poem choices. So, as noted during the Introduction to this section, thinking through potential and productive pairings is a key revision activity – you don't want to have to spend 10 minutes thinking of which partner poem you're going to choose. Think broadly about themes and have a couple of potential connections for each poem. It'll make your exam a lot easier. A similar logic applies to other English Literature exams – think about which bits of the plays or novel you're studying could be used if writing about a particular theme or character. The more you prepare, the easier you'll find the entire process.

> Whilst many poems within the set collection focus on love, pairing Barrett Browning's 'Sonnet 43' with

Rupert Brooke's 'The Soldier' offers an opportunity to explore the ways in which love can offer a form of consolation.[7] Love in both poems is a force of genuine good and both speakers are devoted to the topic of their works, but where for Barrett Browning that's her husband, Robert Browning, for Brooke it's a much larger force, England.

Theme/Paragraph One: Love is used as a way of consolation in both poems to think about and overcome dark events in the past or future.

- From the opening hypophora of 'Sonnet 43' – 'How do I love thee? Let me count the ways.' – Barrett Browning makes clear that love has transformed her life. Despite living under her oppressive[8] father and being disinherited by him following her marriage to Robert Browning, she continues to seek consolation from her love. It is a great source of solace, as suggested by Barrett Browning's use of anaphora – as each answer begins with 'I love thee', the poem builds upon the previous definition, which leaves no doubt to the reader that the love has offered the writer a form of salvation.[9] [*AO1 for incorporating textual references to justify and support an interpretation. AO2 for close analysis of the author's use of form and language. AO3 for demonstrating an understanding of how the context shapes the text*].
- In one of the 'ways', Barrett Browning argues 'I love thee freely, as men strive for Right'. The simile suggests the way in which this love is modest and virtuous, a form of living that rejects all other ways of

being, but also easy and natural, as highlighted by the use of the word 'freely'. [*AO2 for close analysis of the author's use of language.*].
- <u>Pivot to comparison:</u> Both poems are sonnets, a form that's traditionally used in love poetry. Whilst Barrett Browning continues this tradition, for Brooke his use of the sonnet form almost implies the extent of his love of England and the way in which he worships his homeland. The hypothetical[10] situation established at the beginning of the poem, 'If I should die', highlights that the speaker has come to terms with his own mortality and the potential that he might die during the war. There's some solace,[11] however, that in the 'foreign field' (the word 'foreign' illustrates how strange and different it is to England) there will be 'some corner' 'That is forever England.' Brooke's use of the caesura at this point adds an almost celebratory tone to the work, as if England's glory will never be dimmed irrespective of where the speaker is. Thus the speaker's patriotism[12] helps him face any eventuality that awaits him in the near future. [*AO1 for incorporating textual references to justify and support an interpretation. AO2 for close analysis of the author's use of language. AO3 for demonstrating an understanding of how the context shapes the text*].

Theme/Paragraph Two: Where Brooke's poem is an idealised meditation on patriotism, Barrett Browning's work shows genuine emotion for her beloved and how real it can be to love another person.

- War poetry until World War One was often an idealised depiction of patriotism and the desire for glory; however the younger generation of poets like Wilfred Owen challenged the idea that it is a virtue to die for your country. Brooke ignores the terrible trench conditions of the war, reducing them simply to being 'some corner of a foreign field', and he seems to take some solace from the fact that should he die abroad 'There shall be / In that rich earth a richer dust concealed'. In repeating the word 'rich', Brooke's use of the polyptoton[13] celebrates the wealth and value of the English heritage. [*AO1 for incorporating textual references to justify and support an interpretation. AO2 for close analysis of the author's use of form and language*].
- Brooke chooses to focus more on England than wherever he or his fellow soldiers might be posted. England is personified as a rich and bounteous[14] mother figure in the poem: she 'bore, shaped, made aware' the men and gave her 'flowers' to them. England is a place of rest and relaxation, an idyll and image of bliss: 'Washed by the rivers, blest by suns of home.' As pleasant as this is, however, Brooke's idealised patriotism demonstrates how love can be used as a tool to help an individual ignore reality, especially the death and destruction that comes with war. *AO2 for close analysis of the author's use of language. AO3 for demonstrating an understanding of how the context shapes the text*].
- <u>Pivot to comparison:</u> Where it is easy to read Brooke's poem as ignoring the reality around him, Barrett Browning's poem also shows how love can transform a person and occupy their every thought. The sense of

breathless urgency created in the first definition of the speaker's love in lines two and three of 'Sonnet 43' is amplified by the poet's use of enjambment. That she loves Browning to 'the depth and breadth and height / My soul can reach' is further emphasised by the repetition of the word 'and', which in its simplicity becomes almost an ungainly way of outlining such a bold and important topic. [AO2 for close analysis of the author's use of form and language].

Theme/Paragraph Three: Therefore, both Barrett Browning's and Brooke's poems suggest how easy it can be to become devoted to the very thing that you love.

- At the end of 'The Soldier', Brooke focuses on the 'gentleness, / In hearts at peace, under an English heaven.' There is a resounding tone of pride at this closing image of an English paradise. Brooke's love for his country gives him the consolation that dying for England means to have done some good for his country. It is an idyll and a place where memories can be cherished, including the 'dreams happy as her day' and the 'laughter, learnt of friends'. Although some might characterise Brooke's blind devotion as idealistic, it is difficult not to be swept up into his praise, which is made all the more potent by the fact that he would indeed die on a 'foreign field' in Cyprus in 1915 from blood poisoning. At that point, his belief became reality. [AO1 for incorporating textual references to justify and support an interpretation. AO2 for close analysis of the author's use of language.

AO3 for demonstrating an understanding of how the context shapes the text].
- Pivot to comparison: Barrett Browning's devotion to her husband is similarly impressive and evocative. She states she loves him 'with the breath, / Smiles, tears, of all my life!' Barrett Browning places this observation in parenthesis, which gives the lines a zealous[15] urgency. Her love is spiritual and sacred, but it is also of a more human nature: it gives her life and protection, as seen respectively in the line 'by sun and candlelight'. [. *AO2 for close analysis of the author's use of form and language*].
- Barrett Browning's poem reveals her dedication to her husband, a point emphasised through her use of enjambment throughout the poem. In focusing on her 'soul' in line three, it is as if her love is limitless, whilst the capitalisation of certain words like 'Grace', 'Right' and Praise' brings her human love into dialogue with fundamental concepts that define what it means to be human. But more touching of all perhaps is that she loves with a 'childhood's faith', which implies her devotion is innocent and trusting. She is wholly invested in Robert Browning, a point that shines through from the first line of 'Sonnet 43' until the last. [*AO2 for close analysis of the author's use of form and language. AO3 for demonstrating an understanding of how the context shapes the text*].

Conclusion

Sometimes at GCSE level you're asked to comment on things that you might not have given much thought to – for example, I rarely spent my teenage years thinking about marriage, mortality or the power of nature, and I can only assume that you're the same. It can be nice to let your conclusions offer a reflection on the question topic that's emerged from the poems – this way, you're both demonstrating a personal response to the literature and you're showing the examiner that you've taken something away from the poems, which is all we teachers of English Literature ever really want for our students.

"Browning's poem concludes 'I shall but love thee better after death'. The romantic love that Browning feels is eternal, a point that is key to Brooke's patriotic love in 'The Soldier'. Together, these poems suggest how love can console and provide an opportunity to even see death, which should be the end, as a new opportunity for their poets to go on loving that which they hold dear."

A statue of Rupert Brooke in Warwickshire, England.

PAIRING IV: RELATIONSHIPS
'VALENTINE' & 'SHE WALKS IN BEAUTY'

Part a: Read Carol Ann Duffy's 'Valentine'. Duffy's poem is about relationships. How does Duffy present relationships in the poem? Remember to refer to the contexts of the poem in your answer. [15 marks]

INTRODUCTION

"From the beginning of 'Valentine', Carol Ann Duffy makes clear that this is not your usual poem about relationships, but behind the poem's steely tone there is a genuine feeling of love that reminds readers about how wonderful being in a relationship can be."

Theme/Paragraph One: From the beginning of the poem, Duffy takes a cynical[1] but comic approach towards writing about relationships.

- Duffy's poem opens with a single-lined stanza, 'Not a red rose or a satin heart.' The poem was written after Duffy was asked by a radio producer to compose an original poem for Valentine's Day, but from the beginning of 'Valentine' she rejects the traditional images of love, opting instead to give her lover, the poem's addressee, an onion. This comic turn is both at odds with the poem's title, 'Valentine', which implies this will be a love poem, and adds a fresh perspective to the genre of love poetry: onions are sharp and acidic, but they are also layered.[2] As an unexpected extended metaphor[3] for love, then, Duffy uses the onion to explore the complexity of her own feelings. [*AO1 for incorporating textual references to justify and support an interpretation. AO2 for close analysis of the author's use of language. AO3 for demonstrating an understanding of how the context shapes the text*].
- The metaphor 'It is a moon wrapped in brown paper' is another surprising twist, as Duffy moves towards adding an increasing significance to this seemingly unusual choice of topic. The moon, a traditional image of beauty, is here 'wrapped in brown paper', a mundane[4] covering for such a significant entity.[5] Duffy's poem thus early on adopts a tone that uses bathos[6] – it maintains its serious subject of love but focuses on the seemingly trivial[7] onion – to emphasise how this is not a usual poem about relationships. [*AO2 for close analysis of the author's use of language*].

- Although Duffy is cynical about love poems and the various other consumerist[8] representations of love ('Not a cute card or a kissogram'), she states 'I am trying to be truthful.' The first person focus and dramatic monologue[9] form add a strong suggestion that this is a personal reflection on the nature of love. Duffy uses these elements to create a poetic voice that is able to freely express how they feel about love. [*AO2 for close analysis of the author's use of language*].

Theme/Paragraph Two: However, although Duffy's 'Valentine' is keen to almost suggest a lack of sentiment, the poem is deceptive and offers a surprisingly intense portrayal of love.

- There are moments through 'Valentine' where Duffy's tone shifts towards something more serious. For example, after the unusual second stanza, the third stanza begins 'Here.' The short, end-stopped line and sentence is intense. Similarly, the seventh stanza begins 'Take it.', with the short imperative[10] likewise illustrating the speaker's desire for her lover to take this relationship seriously. [*AO1 for incorporating textual references to justify and support an interpretation. AO2 for close analysis of the author's use of form, structure and language*].
- Duffy's poem breaks down the expectations of love poetry, and her work more broadly often subverts[11] and challenges traditional and accepted social forms. Duffy's point in 'Valentine' is partly that love is not so easily defined as the consumerist or materialistic

shops would have readers believe. Instead, Duffy's poem makes it clear that love is irregular and uneven, which is seen in the various stanza lengths used throughout the poem and through Duffy's use of the free verse form.[12] Together, these structural features give the poem a relaxed and conversational feel that together emphasise how this is a modern love poem despite its attempts to camouflage this fact through the unusual opening idea of the onion. [*AO2 for close analysis of the author's use of form and structure. AO3 for demonstrating an understanding of how the context shapes the text*].

- The intensity that slowly comes through Duffy's poem is also achieved through a very subtle use of enjambment. In the second and third stanzas, similes that focus on how the onion can provide more intimate or expected images of love are delayed: for example, 'It will blind you with tears / like a lover.' In delaying these intimate ideas onto the next line, it is as if Duffy's speaker is embarrassed at these moments when she reveals her true feelings, which adds to the idea that this a genuine love poem. [*AO2 for close analysis of the author's use of form, structure and language*].

Conclusion

> "Duffy's 'Valentine' encourages readers to celebrate the ordinary in their relationships. It pushes back against shops and markets that turn love into something that is fully commercial or material. Instead, the ambiguous language used throughout the poem means her speaker

never plainly states the true nature of her feelings; yet underneath this coy[13] game the speaker's attitude towards her partner comes through. She says 'I am trying to be truthful' – her sincerity makes clear that this love poem is more intimate than many others."

A 2008 photo of Carol Ann Duffy at Humber Mouth — a literary festival that took place in Hull, UK. Copyright © Walnut Whippet

Part b: Choose one other poem from the anthology in which the poet also writes about relationships. Compare the way the poet presents relationships in your chosen poem with the way Carol Anne Duffy presents relationships in 'Valentine'. [25 marks]

In your answer you should compare:

• **the content and structure of the poems – what they are about and how they are organised**

• **how the writers create effects, using appropriate terminology where relevant**

• **the contexts of the poems, and how these may have influenced the ideas in them.**

She Walks in Beauty
By Lord Byron

She walks in beauty, like the night
Of cloudless climes and starry skies;
And all that's best of dark and bright
Meet in her aspect and her eyes;
Thus mellowed to that tender light
Which heaven to gaudy day denies.

One shade the more, one ray the less,
Had half impaired the nameless grace

Which waves in every raven tress,
Or softly lightens o'er her face;
Where thoughts serenely sweet express,
How pure, how dear their dwelling-place.

And on that cheek, and o'er that brow,
So soft, so calm, yet eloquent,
The smiles that win, the tints that glow,
But tell of days in goodness spent,
A mind at peace with all below,
A heart whose love is innocent!

Introduction

> "Relationships can be as dangerous as they are wonderful, a point demonstrated by both Duffy's 'Valentine' and Lord Byron's 'She Walks in Beauty'. When placed together, these poems offer an interesting study into how poetry can capture the genuine emotions and feelings an individual goes through when in love and in a relationship, and to what extent this can be an overwhelming feeling."

Theme/Paragraph One: Byron's poem is the very thing Duffy dislikes in 'Valentine': that is, an outpouring of potentially vapid[14] emotion.

- Byron's poem opens with the speaker observing 'She walks in beauty, like the night / Of cloudless climes and starry skies'. The simile emphasises not only the woman's purity but also the atmosphere of mystery that surrounds her. It also establishes a language of light that is used throughout the poem ('tender light' in the first stanza or the 'softly lightens' in stanza two) that explores, celebrates and highlights the woman's radiance. The Romantic poets were fascinated with nature, and here darkness and the night are used as striking reference points to create a figure who is powerful. [*AO1 for incorporating textual references to justify and support an interpretation. AO2 for close analysis of the author's use of language. AO3 for demonstrating an understanding of how the context shapes the text*].

- The poem slowly works through the woman's various features. Byron uses the blazon[15] form, moving from her 'eyes' to her 'face', her 'cheek', her 'brow' and then her 'heart', to illustrate how perfect he finds the woman he's addressing. 'She Walks in Beauty' therefore in part becomes a celebration of female beauty, with the attentiveness with which Byron considers each feature implying his devotion to her. [*AO2 for close analysis of the author's use of form and language. AO3 for demonstrating an understanding of how the context shapes the text*].
- <u>Pivot to comparison:</u> However, although 'She Walks in Beauty' has a tone of genuine admiration, Byron was known for his scandalous relationships and licentious[16] behaviour. As such, it is difficult to fully discern[17] how authentic the poem is. The suggestion of the reality of love poetry is seen in 'Valentine': Duffy was asked to write the poem as an original interpretation of Valentine's Day, and thus she addresses and questions the materialist[18] and

consumerist focus that the day often has in society today. The poem is, as she states in the opening line, 'Not a red rose or a satin heart', nor is it 'a cute card or a kissogram'. It is significant that these are single-lined stanzas, for in using such brief stanzas to note the more common interpretations of Valentine's Day Duffy demonstrates how empty and vacuous[19] these displays of affection are. [*AO2 for close analysis of the author's use of form and language. AO3 for demonstrating an understanding of how the context shapes the text*].

Theme/Paragraph Two: However, underneath the veneer[20] of both poems, there is perhaps a sense of genuine sentiment towards the beloved addressee.

- Byron's poem repeatedly suggests how the addressee of the poem balances light and darkness within her face: it is described in the first stanza how 'all that's best of dark and bright / Meet in her aspect and her eyes'. Bryon admires how the woman's form balances this antithesis. This is also seen in the poem's ABAB rhyme scheme,[21] which is used to represent how these contrasts are naturally brought together in the poem. [*AO1 for incorporating textual references to justify and support an interpretation. AO2 for close analysis of the author's use of form and language*].
- The tone of admiration that comes from 'She Walks in Beauty' is also amplified by the circumstances surrounding its creation: it is thought to have been written about Anne Beatrix Wilmot, Byron's cousin

by marriage, and was published in *Hebrew Melodies*, a 1815 collection of Byron's poetry that was set to music by Isaac Nathan. Despite Byron's rakish[22] reputation, 'She Walks in Beauty' moves beyond physical beauty and towards the suggestion that the woman is as beautiful on the inside as she is on the outside: her 'thoughts serenely sweet express' and her days are 'in goodness spent'. If the poem is based upon Wilmot, then it is clear that Byron feels a great deal of emotion towards her for her entirety, not just her physical looks. [*AO1 for incorporating textual references to justify and support an interpretation. AO3 for demonstrating an understanding of how the context shapes the text*].

- Pivot to comparison: Although Duffy's 'Valentine' opens with a comic suggestion that this is not a typical love poem, as the poem progresses it becomes clear that the speaker cares deeply for their partner. This is achieved in part through the use of the onion as a reference point for the speaker's emotions, which is not dissimilar to how the Metaphysical poets of the seventeenth century used unexpected objects or animals (for example, John Donne's 'The Flea') to suggest their love. Duffy's onion becomes less about its sharp smell and taste and more about how it is guarded and layered. It is unaffected,[23] as highlighted by Duffy's lack of adjectives when describing it, which should be compared with the 'red rose', 'satin heart' or 'cute card' of expected commercialised love. A language of intensity is also used to describe the onion throughout the poem: it 'will blind you', has a 'fierce kiss' and is 'Lethal.' Duffy's onion, therefore, is an impressively versatile[24] extended metaphor that is used to illustrate and celebrate her affection for her partner. [*AO1 for incorporating textual references to justify and support an interpretation. AO2 for close analysis of the author's use of language. AO3 for demonstrating an understanding of how the context shapes the text*].

Theme/Paragraph Three: Regardless of the tone, both poems remind readers of how obsessive love can become.

- Although Byron's poem is more genuine than might be expected from this Romantic poet, the intensity with which he explores each element of the woman is a stark reminder of how exciting, if intense, love and relationships can be. That 'She Walks in Beauty' is written in the present tense adds to the immediacy of the observations made. It is only at the poem's end that Byron explicitly uses the word 'love' – it is as if the poem charts the process an individual goes through when they are infatuated[25] with someone. For all the glory and radiance with which he describes the woman, it is hard not to notice the vigour of Byron's lines as his infatuation is described. [*AO2 for close analysis of the author's use of language. AO3 for demonstrating an understanding of how the context shapes the text*].
- <u>Pivot to comparison:</u> Duffy's poem, by contrast, is much more open about, and directly addresses how, a relationship can become an almost dangerous experience for the individuals involved. The speaker sincerely states 'I am trying to be truthful', reminding the reader that love can be exposing (just as is peeling

away the layers of an onion), a point that is amplified by Duffy's use of the first person in this dramatic monologue. [*AO1 for incorporating textual references to justify and support an interpretation. AO2 for close analysis of the author's use of form and language*].
- At the end of 'Valentine', Duffy describes how the onion's 'scent will cling to your fingers, / cling to your knife'. The repetition of the word 'cling', which as a verb carries connotations of desperation, illustrates the dedication with which the speaker's love will wait until it is reciprocated.[26] At the end of the poem, Duffy emphasises the danger of love, with the word 'knife' being phonetically very similar to the word 'life' – the love shared between two people in a relationship, then, leaves both individuals marked. [*AO2 for close analysis of the author's use of language*].

Conclusion

There's this perception that you shouldn't say anything new in your conclusions. But you want the end of your essay to be lively and engaging. As such, try to get that final bit of analysis in, perhaps save that simple analysis of a simile or word connotation for the end – it's a nice way of maintaining your authority over the work right until the last word and it leaves the examiner feeling that you really know your stuff.

> "Byron's poem makes clear how potent[27] using darkness and the night can be when describing a loved one. As such, Duffy's simile that describes the unusual onion as 'a moon wrapped in brown paper' becomes

more touching and romantic when read alongside Byron's 'She Walks in Beauty'. In both poems, relationships are presented as wonderful things that allow an individual to see the best of another person, although together they also remind readers not to become too infatuated as love can ultimately be dangerous and, as in Duffy's poem, 'Lethal.'"

A bust of Lord Byron.

PAIRING V: MARRIAGE
'COZY APOLOGIA' & 'AFTERNOONS'

Part a: Read Rita Dove's 'Cozy Apologia'. Dove's poem is about marriage. How does Dove present marriage in the poem? Remember to refer to the contexts of the poem in your answer. [15 marks]

INTRODUCTION

Don't forget that you can analyse the titles of the poems in your answer – I do this in the plan below, but also see some thoughts on the titles of Heaney's 'Death of a Naturalist' and Armitage's 'The Manhunt' in the other plans.

"In 'Cozy Apologia', Rita Dove seems somewhat embarrassed by the affection she feels for her husband – the poem puts forward a marriage that seems filled with love and romance, but in which neither participant takes themself too seriously."

Theme/Paragraph One: From the beginning of the poem, Dove's mischievous[1] speaker plays around with her depiction of love.

- Dove's poem opens in a way that readers might expect any love poem to begin. Dove's speaker states 'I could pick anything and think of you', before listing several household objects that admittedly do not naturally make one think of a partner (for example, a lamp or a pen). Yet in the opening stanza, the consistent use of couplets illustrates how the speaker is part of a pairing. That the speaker finds her partner in anything and everything she sees therefore opens the poem with a tone of contentment and joy. [*AO1 for incorporating textual references to justify and support an interpretation. AO2 for close analysis of the author's use of form and language*].
- Yet in 'Cozy Apologia', Dove often avoids any overt[2] sentimentalism.[3] Hence when she thinks about her husband, she characterises him as a medieval knight, 'Astride a dappled mare' and 'with furrowed brow / And chain mail glinting'. This flippant[4] evocation[5] of chivalry[6] of course elevates the husband (he becomes her 'hero') and yet also mocks him. It presents him as suave[7] and elegant but uses hyperbole so that this portrayal is tinged with a tone of irony. Hence from the beginning of the poem Dove creates a tone that celebrates both the love in her marriage and the fun that she has within it.

[*AO2 for close analysis of the author's use of language*].

- With this portrayal of the husband in mind, it might be assumed that the poem is autobiographical. The poem is dedicated 'for Fred', and Dove married the poet Fred Viebahn in 1979. The poem was published in 2003, and so is potentially indicative of the long-term relationship between Dove and Viebahn – it is not quite the intense declaration of love that might be expected from young lovers, and instead reflects more on a relationship that at the point when the poem was published had lasted almost thirty years (the couple met in 1976). The poem presents a happy, content marriage to the point that Dove almost seems embarrassed, hence the title 'Cozy Apologia', which implies that this is a defence of the poet's happiness presumably amidst the destruction of Hurricane Floyd. Dove's use of the dramatic monologue form also adds an element of truth and intimacy to the poem that is seen in the domestic details at the poem's opening. Whilst the opening portrayal of Dove's husband might seem somewhat mocking, then, the poem uses this humour to make clear the affection shared between these two partners. [*AO2 for close analysis of the author's use of form. AO3 for demonstrating an understanding of how the context shapes the text*].

Theme/Paragraph Two: The destructive background of Hurricane Floyd is used to further illustrate how Dove feels about her marriage.

- When Hurricane Floyd landed near North Carolina

in 1999, it caused an immense amount of damage that resulted in 57 fatalities. Yet in 'Cozy Apologia', Dove personifies the hurricane in a way that is surprising: here, it is an almost gentle ('nudging') force that is facetiously[8] called 'Big Bad Floyd'. The hurricane metaphorically 'brings a host / Of daydreams' that for Dove's speaker take her back to childhood crushes. At this point in the poem Dove moves away from the couplets seen earlier, with rhymes now becoming inconsistent – this change subtly captures how 'senseless' these young boys with 'sissy names' are. Dove then describes how these boys 'Were thin as licorice[9] and as chewy', with the simile suggesting how unsubstantial and empty they were; furthermore, this immaturity is suggested through the teasing rhyme of 'Dewey' and 'chewy'. [*AO1 for incorporating textual references to justify and support an interpretation. AO2 for close analysis of the author's use of form and language. AO3 for demonstrating an understanding of how the context shapes the text*].

- Having thought about these young lovers, Dove returns to her partner who is 'bunkered in your / Aerie', which again uses hyperbole to jokingly capture the sense of security he brings to the relationship. As the poem moves towards its conclusion, Dove stresses some concerns about the comfort of the relationship: 'it's embarrassing, this happiness' she observes before asking 'When has the ordinary ever been news?' This rhetorical question highlights the ordinariness of the relationship shared between Dove and her partner but also elevates it so that it becomes an appropriate poetic topic. [*AO2 for close analysis of the author's use of language*].

- And hence why, although there is a tension to stress the fun in Dove's marriage to Fred, the poem ends on a more sentimental note. He keeps her 'from melancholy (call it blues)', with Dove's parenthesis providing a modern definition to a long-standing problem, and she resolves to 'fill this stolen time with you.' The word 'stolen' suggests that the time shared between Dove and her partner is clandestine,[10] but it also carries connotations of value and importance. Dove clearly values the time she has with her husband, a vital fact given the length of their relationship. [*AO2 for close analysis of the author's use of form and language*].

Conclusion

Here again I use the poem to draw a wider conclusion about marriage, something very few know much about at the age of sixteen.

> "Dove might have questioned why her 'ordinary' relationship is worthy of attention, and yet it is clear that a love so unique and enjoyable as that shared between Dove and her husband should be celebrated. At one point Dove admits 'We're content, but fall short of the Divine.' It does not take any form of divine intervention to make it clear that this is a marriage formed of trust and love, which is probably all anyone can hope for."

Part b: Choose one other poem from the anthology in which the poet also writes about marriage. Compare the way the poet presents marriage in your chosen poem with the way Rita Dove presents marriage in 'Cozy Apologia'. [25 marks]

In your answer you should compare:

• **the content and structure of the poems – what they are about and how they are organised**

• **how the writers create effects, using appropriate terminology where relevant**

• **the contexts of the poems, and how these may have influenced the ideas in them.**

Introduction

"Dove's 'Cozy Apologia' and Philip Larkin's 'Afternoons' certainly present two very different ideas of marriage. For the former, marriage offers a chance at happiness; for the latter, marriage presents entrapment and disenchantment.[11] In exploring how these poets both reflect on marriage, readers can identify ways in which they can achieve both happiness and a sense of individualism whilst avoiding future problems like useless husbands and looking back wistfully[12] to the past."

Theme/Paragraph One: Whereas for Dove marriage offers her an escape from the world around her, Larkin continually stresses how marriage has entrapped, and is a detriment to, the young women in the poem.

- Dove's 'Cozy Apologia' opens with a statement: 'I could pick anything and think of you'. The poem's first person and dramatic monologue form together add a sense of intimacy to the work. Indeed, the title suggests that Dove wants to offer a defence for her happy life, a point that is amplified by the dedication 'for Fred'. Throughout the poem, Dove suggests how her marriage, presumably to Fred Viebahn, who she married in 1979, three years after they met in 1976, provides her with happiness. The marriage is distinct from the 'post-post-modern age', the speedy and unrelenting nature of which is illustrated through Dove's use of enjambment in the first three lines of the second stanza, and even 'Big Bad Floyd', a hurricane that is personified as almost gentle. The hurricane gives Dove a chance to think about her husband, and it is a marriage that seems distinctly happy: it is observed, 'We're content, but fall short of the Divine.'[13] Dove's deprecating humour highlights the ordinariness of her married life, but within that she is deeply content. [*AO1 for incorporating textual references to justify and support an interpretation. AO2 for close analysis of the author's use of form and language. AO3 for demonstrating an understanding of how the context shapes the text*].

- <u>Pivot to comparison:</u> Where Dove can see her husband in 'anything' around her, which suggests her happiness at the marriage, Larkin is much more pessimistic about how valuable marriage is. Throughout the first stanza, Larkin's language stresses the sense of emptiness and isolation that these mothers feel. 'Summer', a period of happiness and life, 'is fading', which might symbolically also be read as highlighting how the youth and vigour of the women in the poem is likewise coming to an end; similarly, the 'Young mothers assemble' at the park, with the verb 'assemble' offering a cold and unwelcoming suggestion of this informal group. There is no sense of community or comradery, but instead these mothers are there 'Setting free their children', and whilst this language might initially seem comic, portraying the children as animals, in the context of the rest of the stanza it becomes more about the release that the mothers now feel.[14] Now that their children are gone, there is the suggestion that they can relax. Larkin therefore suggests throughout the first stanza how these mothers live somewhat empty lives. [*AO1 for incorporating textual references to justify and support an interpretation. AO2 for close analysis of the author's use of language*].
- This focus continues throughout the poem, but it is encapsulated in the line 'Their beauty has thickened.' Larkin's metaphor might feel misogynistic,[15] noting that now the women have given birth they have fulfilled their need, yet there is also the suggestion of the sadness behind this immutable change. The word 'thickened' adds a sense of heaviness and inelegance to the mothers, whilst the end-stopped line illustrates

how they cannot go back to the way they were before. As these women age, they become increasingly unable to push back against the social forces that stress how they are no longer valuable or attractive to society, and thus marriage becomes a way of sentencing these young women to a life that is without love. [*AO2 for close analysis of the author's use of form and language*].

Theme/Paragraph Two: In both poems the writers focus on the husbands in the marriages. For Larkin, these men are hollow figures, but Dove writes warmly and comically about her husband, which suggests how intimate their relationship is.

- After stating that 'anything' helps her think of her husband, Dove goes on to describe him with a warmly mocking tone. Leaning on a language of chivalry that evokes an image of a medieval knight, she imagines him 'Astride a dappled mare, legs braced as far apart / As standing in silver stirrups will allow', the sibilance adding a joking, exaggerated tone to the description. This glamorous knight, with his 'chain mail glinting', will have 'One eye smiling, the other firm upon the enemy.' In characterising her husband as a medieval knight, Dove sets him up to be a heroic figure, but the hyperbole surrounding the whole description should not be ignored – through this excessive suggestion of his courageous character, Dove reveals her love for her husband that allows her to semi-seriously present him in such an outlandish and characterful way. [*AO1 for incorporating textual references to justify and support an interpretation. AO2 for close analysis of the author's use of language].*

- Moreover, Dove's husband is drawn into direct comparison with the personified Hurricane Floyd. The hurricane landed in North Carolina in September 1999 and caused flooding and heavy damage; there were 57 fatalities from the storm. This dangerous force of nature however is not quite seen in Dove's poem: instead, 'Big Bad Floyd' is personified as a somewhat less forceful figure who is 'Cussing up a storm.'[16] Because of Floyd, Dove is able to think of her past lovers and her current relationship, the latter of which she writes of affectionately. The changing rhyme scheme of the poem is indicative of Dove's contemplative tone as she considers the theme of love and marriage, which together highlight the intimacy of her relationships. [*AO2 for close analysis of the author's use of form and language. AO3 for demonstrating an understanding of how the context shapes the text*].

- <u>Pivot to comparison:</u> But where Dove's poem is personal and written from personal experience, Larkin never married nor had children, and therefore 'Afternoons' becomes in part a social commentary on the passing of time (and youth) and marriage in the 1950s. The poem offers a window to a period where gender roles were much more heavily defined, where once a woman became a mother, her life became dedicated to ensuring her family unit thrived and was sustained. In 'Afternoons', at the beginning of the second stanza, Larkin focuses on the husbands: 'Behind them, at intervals, / Stand husbands in skilled trades'. The suggestion that these men work 'skilled trades' implies that the mothers are unqualified, and it does not recognise their contribution to the married life shared with these husbands. Furthermore, it is noted that these men are 'Behind' the women (who are plainly but dismissively called 'them') only 'at intervals'. Larkin's use of parenthesis throughout the two caesuras illustrates how fleeting this support is – the suggestion is that they are the "breadwinners" of the family household, but in not fully supporting their wives, these husbands allow them to become empty and without purpose outside of the family unit. [*AO1 for incorporating textual references to justify and support an interpretation. AO2 for close analysis of the author's use of form and language. AO3 for demonstrating an understanding of how the context shapes the text*].

Theme/Paragraph Three: Both poems at some point explore the past lives of the women involved in the marriage, but where in Dove this reminiscence[17] is used for comic effect, there is a direct sense of longing in Larkin's poem for this previous time.

- Larkin's poem has a sparse structure, made up of three octaves without any rhyme scheme. By deploying this structure, Larkin suggests how unromantic the women's lives are – they go about their jobs without complaint but do not lead fulfilling lives. Larkin's poetry often explores the ordinary and the everyday, especially exploring how marriage can impact a couple (which is ironic given that he never married), and yet there is a distinct suggestion of longing that comes throughout the poem. For example, the wedding album, which contains pictures of what is supposed to be the couple's happiest day, is 'lying / Near the television' – the word 'lying' emphasises how it (and the marriage itself) has become disregarded and uncared for. The poem's tone is somewhat uncertain: it might be mocking these women, and Larkin is known for his cynical, ridiculing poetry, and yet the consistency with which he focuses on these women and their now-empty lives encourages readers to consider his tone as potentially being more sympathetic towards these women and the plight that they are now living through. [*AO1 for incorporating textual references to justify and support an interpretation. AO2 for close analysis of the author's use of structure, form and language*].

- As the second stanza moves into the third, Larkin focuses on the 'courting-places' that have become ruined for these women, and yet they are 'still courting-places / (But the lovers are all in school)'. These places symbolise youth, vitality and happiness, but Larkin stresses through the parenthesis how they belong only to the young; the assumption is that the married women are now too old for these places of wanton,[18] childish love. Instead, these mothers must bow to the demands of their children who 'Expect to be taken home.' At the end of 'Afternoons', Larkin highlights that these women are no longer in control of their own lives: 'Something is pushing them / To the side of their own lives', with the ambiguity surrounding 'Something' meaning it is unclear exactly what is enacting such an impressive force on these

women, which simply highlights the tragedy of their loss even more. [*AO2 for close analysis of the author's use of form and language*].
- Pivot to comparison: Where Larkin focuses on the sadness of what has been lost with marriage, Dove is much more open to considering how her previous relationships were with 'worthless boys / Whose only talent was to kiss you senseless.' This simple, uncomplicated love is illustrated through Dove's use of enjambment, which rushes through these lines just as the 'boys' (which implies their immaturity) tried to kiss her. It's when Dove begins to think about these past loves that the rhyming couplet scheme of the poem is broken down – these young loves were all 'hollow' and 'thin as licorice and as chewy', with Dove's simile illustrating how unsubstantial the relationships were. Dove's thinking back to this time is comic, and when compared to her steadfast and gallant husband, these 'sissy' children become all the more immature, suggesting how marriage has provided her with a more fulfilled life. [*AO1 for incorporating textual references to justify and support an interpretation. AO2 for close analysis of the author's use of language*].

Conclusion

Again, it's always nice to give a suggestion of what you've **learned** from this poetry – the poems have been chosen to get you thinking more broadly about not only literature, but life and the world around you. Give the exam board a little of what they want in your conclusion – it certainly gives the impression that you're a receptive reader and student.

"In reading Larkin's 'Afternoons' in dialogue with Dove's 'Cozy Apologia', it becomes apparent to these young eyes that marriage is what you make of it. Larkin's cynicism might offer a warning to young people, but the genuine sense of feeling that radiates from Dove's poem is hard to ignore. Dove's poem ends with a focus on intimacy: 'I fill this stolen time with you.' The word 'stolen' adds a suggestion of how this love is clandestine, secret and special – if you have found the right partner, hopefully every moment will feel this way."

A 1999 photo of a toppled rocket at Cape Canaveral, Florida — illustrative of the damage wrought by Hurricane Floyd (the hurricane alluded to in Dove's poem!).

PAIRING VI: INNOCENCE
'THE PRELUDE' & 'DEATH OF A NATURALIST'

Part a: Read William Wordsworth's excerpt from *The Prelude*. Wordsworth's poem is about innocence. How does Wordsworth present innocence in the poem? Remember to refer to the contexts of the poem in your answer. [15 marks]

Except from The Prelude
William Wordsworth

And in the frosty season, when the sun
Was set, and visible for many a mile
The cottage windows through the twilight blaz'd,
I heeded not the summons: – happy time
It was, indeed, for all of us; to me
It was a time of rapture: clear and loud
The village clock toll'd six; I wheel'd about,

Proud and exulting, like an untir'd horse,
That cares not for his home. – All shod with steel,
We hiss'd along the polish'd ice, in games
Confederate, imitative of the chase
And woodland pleasures, the resounding horn,
The Pack loud bellowing, and the hunted hare.
So through the darkness and the cold we flew,
And not a voice was idle; with the din,
Meanwhile, the precipices rang aloud,
The leafless trees, and every icy crag
Tinkled like iron, while the distant hills
Into the tumult sent an alien sound
Of melancholy, not unnoticed, while the stars,
Eastward, were sparkling clear, and in the west
The orange sky of evening died away.

INTRODUCTION

It's worth remember that Wordsworth's The Prelude is a long, epic poem (as in, it belongs to the epic genre, but that's not to say it isn't pretty great). Try, if you can, to make sure you refer to this work as an **excerpt**, just to show your examiner that you're aware that it's from a longer piece.

> "The excerpt from William Wordsworth's *The Prelude* reminds readers of the blissful joy and innocence that come with childhood. Describing a time he went ice skating as a child, Wordsworth explores and reflects on his previous innocence, in part using nature as a frame to consider what he has now lost in adulthood."

PAIRING VI: INNOCENCE 79

Theme/Paragraph One: At the beginning of the extract, Wordsworth presents a nostalgic[1] tone for his childhood and captures how idyllic and exciting this innocent time was.

- At the beginning of the excerpt, Wordsworth describes the encroaching[2] darkness during this 'frosty season'; it is described how 'the twilight blaz'd' through 'cottage windows', with the word 'blaz'd' suggesting how vibrant and exciting this time was and how warmly Wordsworth thinks about this time of childhood. This focus on the liveliness of this time is also seen when Wordsworth describes this period as 'a time of rapture',[3] which illustrates the ecstasy he felt during these younger years. [*AO1 for incorporating textual references to justify and support an interpretation. AO2 for close analysis of the author's use of language*].
- Many of the verbs throughout the excerpt highlight the unfaltering energy with which the young Wordsworth played with his friends. He 'wheel'd about', which suggests the rapid movement, and 'hiss'd along the polish'd ice'. These movements are all captured together in the simile 'Proud and exulting, like an untir'd horse' – through this simile, Wordsworth emphasises the strength and energy he felt at this moment whilst also registering the freedom that comes with childhood. The description is also amplified by Wordsworth's use of the first person, which, whilst retrospective, adds a tone of nostalgia to the work, setting this period of the poet's life as one of

idyllic 'rapture'. [*AO2 for close analysis of the author's use of language*].

- Wordsworth continued to find joy in ice skating throughout his life – as a father, he pulled his children in a basket across the ice. In this excerpt, there is a similar suggestion of how freeing ice skating is; it is likened to the 'woodland pleasures' of a royal hunt ('the resounding horn' and 'the hunted hare'). This description elevates the ice skating – it becomes something exciting, full of adventure and belonging to the chivalric courts[4] of the medieval period. It is an activity that keeps the young Wordsworth warm both literally and symbolically as 'through the darkness and the cold we flew', with the verb 'flew' carrying connotations of both speed and freedom. The central description of ice skating in the excerpt, then, encapsulates[5] the energy of childhood, whilst conveying a clear longing to return to this period of uncomplicated happiness. [*AO1 for incorporating textual references to justify and support an interpretation. AO2 for close analysis of the author's use of language*].

Theme/ Paragraph Two: As the excerpt continues, Wordsworth uses nature as a frame to retrospectively explore the passing of his childhood innocence.

- Like other Romantic poets, Wordsworth shows a clear respect for the power of nature; however, he also found personal solace in the natural world, especially in the Lake District, following the deaths of both his parents before he was 13. In the excerpt, it is as if the countryside has come alive ('the precipices rang aloud'). The line 'every icy crag / Tinkled like iron' adds an element of delicacy to this harsh environment ('Tinkled') and brings it into contrast with the tolling village clock.[6] [*AO2 for close analysis of the author's use of language. AO3 for demonstrating an understanding of how the context shapes the text*].

- In the second half of the excerpt, Wordsworth turns somewhat more seriously to reflect upon the distance between humans and nature, which he also uses to reflect a sadness for his lost childhood. The hills emit 'an alien sound / Of melancholy', adding a slight tone of protest to what has until this point in the extract been a poem of celebration. As a retrospective account of childhood events, this 'melancholy' suggests Wordsworth's thinking about these days of innocence has become tinged with sadness, with the use of enjambment very slightly suggesting how this sadness is a new, more mature voice that contrasts with the childish delight ('the din'). This melancholy is parenthetically noted as being 'not unnoticed' – the younger Wordsworth did recognise the sound, but did not fully appreciate or understand its significance. [*AO1 for incorporating textual references to justify and support an interpretation. AO2 for close analysis of the author's use of form and language*].

- The autobiographical element of *The Prelude,* which is a retelling of Wordsworth's life within the genre of epic poetry,[7] adds a much deeper level of introspection[8] to the poem. Although the first person voice of the poem fades towards the end of the extract, there is still something quite striking about the way in which the older poet interjects[9] into the narrative. This is also seen in the language used to describe the nature around Wordsworth, which balances youth and vibrancy ('sparkling clear') with a symbolic focus on death and ending ('The orange sky of evening died away.'). However, the various caesuras in this description of nature add an admiring tone to the work – Wordsworth appreciates the world around him and uses it to reflect positively on his own childhood. [*AO2 for close analysis of the author's use of form and language. AO3 for demonstrating an understanding of how the context shapes the text*].

Conclusion

"As might be expected from one of the most famous Romantic poets, Wordsworth's exploration of innocence in this excerpt from The Prelude is rooted in the natural world. Nature becomes a frame for pondering how childhood innocence can slip away and yet it is impossible to ignore the tone of nostalgia and delight with which Wordsworth writes about his earlier years. Referring to the signs that he should go home, Wordsworth observes 'I heeded not the summons' – this naughty behaviour shows a lust for life that all adults would do well to listen to and try to recreate when the weight of later years feels too much."

Part b: Choose one other poem from the anthology in which the poet also writes about innocence. Compare the way the poet presents innocence in your chosen poem with the way William Wordsworth presents innocence in the excerpt from *The Prelude*. [25 marks]

In your answer you should compare:

• **the content and structure of the poems – what they are about and how they are organised**

• **how the writers create effects, using appropriate terminology where relevant**

• **the contexts of the poems, and how these may have influenced the ideas in them.**

Introduction

"Alongside the excerpt from Wordsworth's *The Prelude*, Seamus Heaney's 'Death of a Naturalist' offers similar lessons about innocence. Both poets focus on childhood joy that is tinged with the knowledge that comes with experience. Using nature as a frame, innocence becomes a fleeting state that must be cherished and protected."

Theme/Paragraph One: Both Heaney and Wordsworth begin their poems by expressing a sense of joy within their childhood memories.

- For Heaney, there is a surprisingly earthy pleasure and enthusiasm for the language of rot and disease ('rotted' and 'sweltered'), which illustrates how the poet is thinking back to his earlier years and the joy that is often present in children for gross things. Growing up on a farm in Northern Ireland, Heaney was certainly familiar with the dirty reality of rural life, and it is clear in this poem that he enjoys this space. Although the sun is personified ('punishing') in a way that suggests how oppressive it is, the 'Bubbles gargled delicately' in the water, with Heaney's oxymoron highlighting the enjoyment his younger self felt amidst this environment. It is a place of 'dragon-flies' and 'spotted butterflies'. The frogspawn is described as 'warm thick slobber', which 'grew like clotted water'; Heaney's simile and language should portray this space negatively — it should be repellent[10] and disgusting — and yet there is a joy amidst this natural world in part because of the way in which it reminds him of his childhood. [*AO1 for incorporating textual references to justify and support an interpretation. AO2 for close analysis of the author's use of language. AO3 for demonstrating an understanding of how the context shapes the text*].
- Furthermore, later on in the first stanza Heaney relocates the poem's setting to a school classroom. 'Miss Walls' teaches her students about 'daddy' and 'mammy' frogs — throughout this section, Heaney deliberately uses childish language to imply the age

and immaturity of his speaker at this point. When it is described how the frogspawn 'burst into nimble- / Swimming tadpoles', there is a sense of excitement and energy through the verb 'burst', whilst the enjambment captures the elegance of these new-born creatures. The poem's first-person narrator and use of blank verse together add a conversational tone to the poem, with the lack of rhyme adding an element of simplicity that is indicative of Heaney's self-presentation of being a younger age. Through this memory, then, Heaney again suggests his innocence and how happy that made him – it was a simpler time when he could explore his interests in the natural world without an awareness of how it might impact him in the future. [*AO1 for incorporating textual references to justify and support an interpretation. AO2 for close analysis of the author's use of form and language*].

- <u>Pivot to comparison:</u> Wordsworth similarly describes his earlier childhood years with a tone of nostalgia and happiness. For example, there is a vivacity to the town in which he lives, as seen in the description of how the 'twilight blaz'd', which highlights how lively and excitable this time was and suggests how Wordsworth thinks warmly about his earlier years. Wordsworth describes this period as 'a time of rapture', adding an intense suggestion of ecstasy to the description that is then seen through the strong use of verbs: 'wheel'd' suggests how energic and rapid the movements are and the onomatopoeic 'hiss'd' to describe the ice-skating adds a sharp precision that illustrates how fast he is moving. Wordsworth describes himself 'like an untir'd horse' – the simile emphasises how strong and free he was during this time. Through these various language techniques, then, Wordsworth effectively creates an excitable and appreciative tone for his earlier innocence. [*AO1 for incorporating textual references to justify and support an interpretation. AO2 for close analysis of the author's use of form and language*].

Theme/ Paragraph Two: However both poems have voltas[11] where they move from innocence to experience and a tone of fear accompanies this change.

- The title of Heaney's poem is symbolic. It is also the name of Heaney's first collection of poetry, which was published in 1966 – this collection often explores ideas of innocence, growing up and identity.[12] These themes are all seen in this poem. In calling himself a 'Naturalist', Heaney uses a child-like hyperbole to elevate his position: the poem focuses on his early years at school. He's not a formal 'Naturalist', merely an interested pupil. However, as noted through the use of the word 'Death' in the title, Heaney's interest will be replaced with an awareness of the ugly reality of the natural world around him. [*AO2 for close analysis of the author's use of language. AO3 for demonstrating an understanding of how the context shapes the text*].
- The volta of Heaney's poem marks the change in tone. It is noted quite simply and bluntly ('Then') and describes a similar scene to what is seen at the beginning of the poem by focusing on the swamp-like

space. However, where before there was a tone of enjoyment when Heaney described this place, now it has become dangerous to him, as suggested by the use of military language throughout the second stanza. For example, angry frogs have 'Invaded' with their 'coarse croaking'. Some are sat 'Poised like mud grenades' – Heaney's simile again adds a tone of danger to these animals. The frog's hopping is described using the onomatopoeic words 'slap and plop', which before in their comic hyperbole might have suggested a childish revelling in the grossness of the actions but now they have become serious, 'obscene threats'. Heaney's interpretation of nature has changed, and with his experience there is now a danger in this festering world. [*AO2 for close analysis of the author's use of structure and language*].

- <u>Pivot to comparison:</u> Where Heaney seems to have become fearful of the world around him, for Wordsworth there is a sadness at the realisation that his childhood has passed. Wordsworth writes of how 'the distant hills / Into the tumult sent an alien sound / Of melancholy, not unnoticed'. The use of the word 'alien' illustrates how this is unfamiliar and unusual for the young Wordsworth, but he also notes how this sound was 'not unnoticed' – it is as if the young Wordsworth could not appreciate the feeling of 'melancholy' that was hanging in the hills around him but as an adult he recognises this feeling and is now familiar with it. [*AO1 for incorporating textual references to justify and support an interpretation. AO2 for close analysis of the author's use of language*].

Theme/Paragraph Three: A key element of both poems is the way in which nature is used as an effective frame to explore how innocence slowly disappears.

- The Romantic poets are known for their deep respect for nature, which is seen during the excerpt of Wordsworth's The Prelude. Wordsworth in particular found comfort in nature following the death of both parents before he was 13. Wordsworth's use of the first person at the beginning of the excerpt emphasises both the retrospective quality of his account and the tone of nostalgia that he attaches to the description of nature. Set amidst the gathering darkness, Wordsworth uses nature to explore his childhood. This is a nature that comes alive ('the precipices rang aloud') and is unexpectedly pretty at points. For example, 'every icy crag / Tinkled like iron'. Amidst the unrelenting cold of the environment, the verb 'Tinkled' and the simile together add an element of delicacy to this noise. [*AO2 for close analysis of the author's use of language. AO3 for demonstrating an understanding of how the context shapes the text*].
- More generally, towards the end of the excerpt Wordsworth shows his appreciation of nature through his heavy use of caesuras: 'while the stars, / Eastward, were sparkling clear'. In slowing the pace, there is a sense of respect for nature's majesty, with the verb 'sparkling' highlighting the youthful vivacity of the stars. At the end of the poem, it is described how 'The orange sky of evening died away' – this vivid sunset symbolically notes both the end of the day and the

end of Wordsworth's childhood innocence. Nature therefore is used in a way that is typical of the Romantic period, with Wordsworth's intensely personal poem becoming a moving evocation of the changes that come with growing older. [*AO2 for close analysis of the author's use of form and language. AO3 for demonstrating an understanding of how the context shapes the text*].

- <u>Pivot to comparison:</u> Heaney's younger brother died aged 4 in 1953 when Heaney was in his early teenage years. It can be inferred then that Heaney was starkly aware of how innocence is lost, which is felt particularly throughout this poem. What is most striking is the way in which the familiar natural world soon becomes overwhelming for Heaney. He describes in the second stanza how the 'coarse croaking' was a sound 'that I had not heard / Before.' Heaney's use of enjambment here captures that sense of discovery – like the line, he is turning into the unknown – and yet it is cut short by the caesura. At the end of the poem, Heaney observes 'I sickened, turned, and ran.' This simple, short sentence offers a sharp contrast to the earlier excitement seen in the poem and illustrates the speed with which Heaney's speaker attempts to leave the space that was once so comforting. [*AO1 for incorporating textual references to justify and support an interpretation. AO2 for close analysis of the author's use of form and language. AO3 for demonstrating an understanding of how the context shapes the text*].

Conclusion

Again, exploring the end of a poem can be a fruitful and simple way of ending your essay. The more you practice, the easier it will become.

"At the end of Heaney's poem, nature becomes a force of terrifying power, with those 'great slime kings' who were once the focus of child-like joy and fascination becoming cruel and vengeful tyrants. Wordsworth and Heaney together suggest the importance of maintaining one's childhood innocence. In reading both poems, it becomes clear that innocence gives a person a joyous naivety with which they can enjoy everything around them. To lose that innocence, then, marks the beginning of a new way of viewing the world that is filled with fear and anxiety."

Seamus Heaney at University College Dublin, 2009.

PAIRING VII: PLACE
'LONDON' & 'LIVING SPACE'

Part a: Read William Blake's 'London'. Blake's poem is about a place. How does Blake present the place in the poem? Remember to refer to the contexts of the poem in your answer. [15 marks]

London
By William Blake

I wander thro' each charter'd street,
Near where the charter'd Thames does flow.
And mark in every face I meet
Marks of weakness, marks of woe.

In every cry of every Man,
In every Infants cry of fear,
In every voice: in every ban,

The mind-forg'd manacles I hear

How the Chimney-sweepers cry
Every blackning Church appalls,
And the hapless Soldiers sigh
Runs in blood down Palace walls

But most thro' midnight streets I hear
How the youthful Harlots curse
Blasts the new-born Infants tear
And blights with plagues the Marriage hearse

Introduction

> "As the speaker of William Blake's 'London' walks through the city named in the poem's title, he cannot help but be overwhelmed by the apparent poverty and difficulty that many faced in Industrial London."

Theme/Paragraph One: Throughout the poem, Blake is disgusted by the oppression everyone he comes across is facing on a daily basis.

- In the first line, Blake describes the streets as 'charter'd',[1] a word that is repeated in the second line. Blake originally wrote 'dirty street' in the first line. For something to be 'chartered' means public land was placed under private ownership. In actively choosing this word, then, Blake highlights how the difficulty he is observing has become fixed and rigid, focusing more on social oppression than on the condition of the streets [*AO1 for incorporating textual references to justify and support an interpretation. AO2 for close analysis of the author's use of language. AO3 for demonstrating an understanding of how the context shapes the text*].

- Moreover, in the second stanza Blake uses anaphora ('In every') to begin the first three lines, which all focus on how the people of London are suffering (which is also illustrated by the repetition of 'cry'). Blake uses the repetition to highlight the enormity of the poverty he sees all around him, which creates an overall bleak tone to the poem. [*AO1 for incorporating textual references to justify and support an interpretation. AO2 for close analysis of the author's use of language. AO3 for demonstrating an understanding of how the context shapes the text*].
- Finally, at the end of the second stanza Blake describes how the poorest of the city's inhabitants wear 'mind-forg'd manacles'.[2] This metaphor emphasises how these people are trapped by their situation, a point that is exaggerated through the use of the word 'manacles'. Blake had initially written 'mind-forg'd links', but in using the word 'manacles' he introduces the connotation of prisons and entrapment more directly, thus making the oppression all the clearer for the reader. [*AO2 for close analysis of the author's use of language. AO3 for demonstrating an understanding of how the context shapes the text*].

Theme/Paragraph Two: Blake is frustrated by the lack of support from those key institutions that

are supposed to provide for people and cultivate liveable places.

- 'London' is an intensely personal poem: Blake lived in London and knew of the city's issues intimately, which is also suggested by the use of the first person pronoun from the poem's beginning ('I wander'). Industrial London was dirty and corrupt, with poverty and overcrowding common throughout large areas of the city. Indeed, at the end of the poem Blake uses a language of illness ('blights with plagues') to suggest how infectious this corruption has become. [*AO2 for close analysis of the author's use of language. AO3 for demonstrating an understanding of how the context shapes the text*].
- Blake uses oxymorons in the second half of the poem to suggest how the city is full of contradictions and disappointments. The 'black'ning Church' implies how this institution that should offer charity has become corrupt, whilst the idea of a 'youthful Harlot' juxtaposes the supposed optimism of childhood with the blunt statement that this girl is a prostitute. [*AO2 for close analysis of the author's use of language*].
- Despite Blake's anger at how these institutions do not support the people, there's the suggestion that little will change in the near future. Blake's regular ABAB rhyme scheme and structured use of quatrains highlights how this suffering is now locked into place with little hope of change coming soon. [*AO2 for close analysis of the author's use of form and structure.*]

Conclusion

"Industrial London was a difficult, unforgiving place to live in, and Blake makes it very clear throughout 'London' why this was. It is hard not to be sympathetic to the suffering of the young chimney sweepers or 'youthful Harlots' and throughout the poem Blake's focus on hearing the suffering of those around ('cry', 'sighs', 'curse') emphasises how one place can quickly become hell on earth if poverty and inequality are not stopped."

A reproduction of Blake's hand-painted print that he published alongside the poem in 1826.

Part b: Choose one other poem from the anthology in which the poet also writes about places. Compare the way the poet presents relationships in your chosen poem with the way William Blake presents a place in 'London'. [25 marks]

In your answer you should compare:

• **the content and structure of the poems – what they are about and how they are organised**

• **how the writers create effects, using appropriate terminology where relevant**

• **the contexts of the poems, and how these may have influenced the ideas in them.**

Introduction

"Both Blake's 'London and Imtiaz Dharker's 'Living Space' suggest how poverty can become the defining quality of a person, leading to the realisation that a place can exert a power over an individual. However, where Blake implies that nothing can be done, Dharker is somewhat hopeful for those living in the slums of Mumbai. The distinctive places in both poems, then, although different in culture and geography, together suggest how important it is for oppressed people to continue fighting to keep their identity."

Theme/Paragraph One: The harsh and unacceptable living conditions depicted in both poems are stark reminders of how poverty can almost be crippling.

- Nineteenth-century London was dirty and corrupt: The Industrial Revolution meant that large factories employed children to work dangerous machinery, with smoke and smog everywhere. Blake's 'London' uses oxymorons ('black'ning Church', 'youthful Harlot' and 'Marriage hearse') to highlight how the city is a place of corruption and difficulty, the effect of which has left a 'mark in every face' Blake's speaker comes across. Blake contrasts the physical 'marks of weakness', which suggest illness or suffering, with the metaphorical 'marks of woe' at the end of the first stanza – those who live in Blake's London are crippled by their poverty. [*AO1 for incorporating textual references to justify and support an interpretation. AO2 for close analysis of the author's use of language. AO3 for demonstrating an understanding of how the context shapes the text*].
- Indeed, the metaphor that the poor inhabitants of London wear 'mind-forg'd manacles' further emphasises this point. Blake's metaphor illustrates how the social hierarchy ensures that those at the bottom stay there, with the entrenched class system offering little opportunity for others to break these restrictions – that they are 'mind-forg'd' emphasises how these people do not believe they can do better in life and thus will stay in this state of purgatory

forever. [*AO2 for close analysis of the author's use of language*].

- <u>Pivot to comparison:</u> Dharker's poem is likewise unforgiving in its representation of the difficult living conditions in the slums of India. The poem's title, 'Living Space', is an ironic reflection of how dangerous it is there – as described in the first stanza, 'Nothing is flat / or parallel', with the enjambment hinting at how regular boundaries have been removed. Similarly, it is described how 'Nails clutch at open seams', with Dharker's personification and the use of the word 'clutch' indicating the desperation of the buildings just to remain standing. To live in poverty, as suggested by both poems, means to live in a state of desperation. [*AO1 for incorporating textual references to justify and support an interpretation. AO2 for close analysis of the author's use of form and language. AO3 for demonstrating an understanding of how the context shapes the text*].

Theme/Paragraph Two: Together, the two poems show how places can have a heavy influence on, and power over, the lives of those who live within their confines.

- Blake's poem opens with the speaker walking through 'each charter'd street'. In using the word 'charter'd' and not, as written in an original draft, 'dirty', Blake focuses more on the process by which power dynamics between the upper and lower classes are cemented. Indeed, the regular structure of 'London' – the ABAB rhyme scheme and consistent quatrains –

also suggests how the bleak conditions and suffering are unlikely to change. [*AO1 for incorporating textual references to justify and support an interpretation. AO2 for close analysis of the author's use of language. AO3 for demonstrating an understanding of how the context shapes the text*].

- <u>Pivot to comparison:</u> Where Blake talks about how the streets are 'charter'd', Dharker's poem opens with the statement 'There are just not enough / straight lines' – the problems with the building in front of her is that its structure is unordered. Dharker's use of adverbs in the first stanza suggests how unsafe this area is – the beams are 'crookedly on supports', and the 'whole structure leans dangerously'. Amidst this environment, as noted in the second stanza, 'someone has squeezed / a living space' – the compactness of this stanza (three lines) versus that of the first and third stanzas (ten and nine lines respectively)[3] truly illustrates how the living space has been 'squeezed' in, which would have an inevitable impact on those who live there. [*AO1 for incorporating textual references to justify and support an interpretation. AO2 for close analysis of the author's use of structure and language. AO3 for demonstrating an understanding of how the context shapes the text*].
- Although she was raised in Scotland, Dharker was born in Pakistan; she is interested in representing different cultures and often draws on her own multi-cultural experience in her work. Her intimate knowledge of Mumbai and the living conditions there comes through in this poem, as seen for example in the free verse metre and frequent enjambment throughout the poem, which together suggest how

there are no boundaries in this space. [*AO3 for demonstrating an understanding of how the context shapes the text*].

Theme/Paragraph Three: Blake's tone is solely pessimistic,[4] as if he has become infected by the suffering around him, but Dharker sees some potential and hope in Mumbai.

- By the end of 'London', Blake's anger at the inequality around him is clear. His enjambment across the second, third and fourth stanzas illustrates how incessant the list of difficulties is, with the almost apocalyptic[5] language ('blood down Palace walls' and 'blights with plagues') adding to this sense of hopelessness. This bleak tone is amplified through Blake's use of the first person at the beginning of the poem ('I wander') – this is a personal, angry response to what surrounds Blake as he lives in the industrial smog of London. [*AO1 for incorporating textual references to justify and support an interpretation. AO2 for close analysis of the author's use of form and language. AO3 for demonstrating an understanding of how the context shapes the text*].
- <u>Pivot to comparison:</u> Where Dharker's poem opens in a somewhat more detached, descriptive voice – she quickly diagnoses 'That / is the problem.' – as the poem continues she becomes more invested in the hope and persistence of the people who live in India. This thought is introduced when she spots some 'eggs in a wire basket' that someone has 'dared' to place there. There's something of a tone of awe about these

'fragile curves of white' – the eggs are symbolic of not only vulnerability but also of faith and new opportunity. [*AO2 for close analysis of the author's use of language*].
- The eggs prompt Dharker to think with a tentative[6] hopefulness about this place – it is a place where 'light' can be gathered and the eggs are described as having 'bright, thin walls of faith.' Although 'bright' is suggestive of happiness and 'faith' is a worthy quality to have, the walls are described as 'thin'. Again, this happiness is frail, but there is something special about this injection of life amidst the chaos of the city, and Dharker seems to take great hope in this final image about the precarious insistence of an individual's right to live. [*AO1 for incorporating textual references to justify and support an interpretation. AO2 for close analysis of the author's use of language*].

Conclusion

> "Blake struggles against the inequalities of London, a place that has become corrupt through wealth and the abuse of power. For Dharker, however, the persistence of people to live amidst such disruption is a source of inspiration. Despite the ironic title, it is significant that both the first and third stanzas begin with a focus on faith – it is indeed nothing short of 'miraculous', as Dharker puts it, that people will always assert their right to live even in the hardest of circumstances."

PAIRING VIII: NATURE
'AS IMPERCEPTIBLY AS GRIEF' & 'TO AUTUMN'

Part a: Read Emily Dickinson's 'As Imperceptibly as Grief'. Dickinson's poem is about nature. How does Dickinson present nature in the poem? Remember to refer to the contexts of the poem in your answer. [15 marks]

As Imperceptibly as Grief
By Emily Dickinson

As imperceptibly as Grief
The Summer lapsed away —
Too imperceptible at last
To seem like Perfidy —

A Quietness distilled

As Twilight long begun,
Or Nature spending with herself
Sequestered Afternoon —

The Dusk drew earlier in —
The Morning foreign shone —
A courteous, yet harrowing Grace,
As Guest, that would be gone —

And thus, without a Wing
Or service of a Keel
Our Summer made her light escape
Into the Beautiful.

Introduction

"In 'As Imperceptibly as Grief', Emily Dickinson uses nature as a way of framing her own thoughts and considerations about death and passing happiness. However in this quiet, contemplative poem readers can also identify a respect for the natural process of time and what this brings for humans."

Theme/Paragraph One: Throughout the poem Dickinson personifies nature as a way of expressing her own fears and grief.

- From the poem's opening, Dickinson sets up nature as a way of writing about her own fears and concerns, a theme that is present throughout her poetry. For example, in describing how the summer 'lapsed away', Dickinson adds an almost passive quality to it, which is further suggested by how it is 'Too imperceptible at last / To seem like Perfidy'. This passing is so gentle, it appears to be honest, not deceiving or treacherous ('Perfidy'), and yet at the same time it is as if nature has tricked Dickinson's speaker. [*AO1 for incorporating textual references to justify and support an interpretation. AO2 for close analysis of the author's use of language*].
- Similarly, the ABCB rhyme scheme of the poem both stresses resonance and change – although some words are matched through rhyme, other words are alone and disconnected. This form then highlights how nothing is regular and the world is changing, which Dickinson seems to find simultaneously unsettling and comforting as nature takes its usual course. [*AO2 for close analysis of the author's use of form*].
- Indeed, whilst the end of summer carries a mixed tone for Dickinson, when she moves towards a more autumnal period, or more broadly a period of change as highlighted in line six 'As Twilight long begun', nature is personified as something comfortable and peaceful. She is 'spending with her / Sequestered Afternoon'. Dickinson therefore uses nature as a way of writing about the anxieties that come with change, which is prompted by her own concerns about grief. [*AO1 for incorporating textual references to justify and support an interpretation. AO2 for close analysis of the author's use of language*].

Theme/Paragraph Two: In the second half of the poem, Dickinson focuses more on how nature can represent change.

- The dashes that are so typical to Dickinson's poetic style here present brief pictures of different parts of nature in action: for example, 'The Dusk drew earlier in' or 'The Morning foreign shone'. These brief glimpses of change cumulatively build up so that by the end it is difficult not to be overwhelmed by how powerful change is. [*AO2 for close analysis of the author's use of form and language*].
- This focus on change is also seen in a number of oxymorons: for example, the 'Morning' has 'A courteous, yet harrowing Grace', which suggests that things that should be enjoyable and pleasant can easily become unsettling. The simile is also described as a 'Guest, that would be gone'. Dickinson's simile illustrates how everything must come to an end. This mixed focus on nature is certainly indicative of the life of isolation that the poet lived – there is a sense throughout this poem of how Dickinson long meditated on nature and the brevity of happiness. As a social recluse, Dickinson obviously had a lot of time to contemplate the world around her, hence the quiet, intimate and surprising implications of much of this poem. [*AO2 for close analysis of the author's use of language. AO3 for demonstrating an understanding of how the context shapes the text*].
- And yet, despite the uncertainty that comes through the poem, at the end there is something celebratory

about the final image of summer's 'escape / Into the Beautiful.' This may then suggest how Dickinson's own grief has been somewhat abated by the reflections on the indomitable process of the seasons. In part, this is achieved through Dickinson's use of enjambment in the final four lines of the poem that is unbroken by the dashes seen earlier in the poem, which captures this final burst of poetic inspiration and realisation. Nature, then, gives Dickinson a way of not only writing about change but also reconciling[1] herself to it. [*AO1 for incorporating textual references to justify and support an interpretation. AO2 for close analysis of the author's use of form, structure and language. AO3 for demonstrating an understanding of how the context shapes the text*].

Conclusion

Contextual readings are fine, but it's not always good to base all of your analysis on them. Sometimes the curtains are just blue, and they don't mean the writer was depressed. But, again, acknowledging the way in which these slightly more obvious readings can be nuanced can be a sound way of concluding your essay, as again it shows a level of maturity in your thinking.

> "It is perhaps easy to read Dickinson's 'As Imperceptibly as Grief' as a reflection of the poet's own solitary life. Living alone in rural America, Dickinson would no doubt have had opportunities to look outside her window and consider what the landscape meant to her.

And yet this elegy[2] for summer ends on a comforting note, with the word 'escape' in particular reflecting something of a celebration of nature's beauty. The poem reminds us that although grief can have a devastating effect, it is, just like nature, something that will pass and change."

An 1847 daguerreotype of Emily Dickinson.

Part b: Choose one other poem from the anthology in which the poet also writes about nature. Compare the way the poet presents nature in your chosen poem with the way Emily Dickinson presents nature in 'As Imperceptibly as Grief'. [25 marks]

In your answer you should compare:

- **the content and structure of the poems – what they are about and how they are organised**

- **how the writers create effects, using appropriate terminology where relevant**

- **the contexts of the poems, and how these may have influenced the ideas in them.**

To Autumn
By John Keats

Season of mists and mellow fruitfulness,
  Close bosom-friend of the maturing sun;
Conspiring with him how to load and bless
  With fruit the vines that round the thatch-eves run;
To bend with apples the moss'd cottage-trees,
  And fill all fruit with ripeness to the core;
    To swell the gourd, and plump the hazel shells
  With a sweet kernel; to set budding more,
And still more, later flowers for the bees,
Until they think warm days will never cease,

           For summer has o'er-brimm'd their clammy cells.

       Who hath not seen thee oft amid thy store?
          Sometimes whoever seeks abroad may find
       Thee sitting careless on a granary floor,
          Thy hair soft-lifted by the winnowing wind;
       Or on a half-reap'd furrow sound asleep,
          Drows'd with the fume of poppies, while thy hook
             Spares the next swath and all its twined flowers:
       And sometimes like a gleaner thou dost keep
          Steady thy laden head across a brook;
          Or by a cyder-press, with patient look,
             Thou watchest the last oozings hours by hours.

       Where are the songs of spring? Ay, Where are they?
          Think not of them, thou hast thy music too,—
       While barred clouds bloom the soft-dying day,
          And touch the stubble-plains with rosy hue;
       Then in a wailful choir the small gnats mourn
          Among the river sallows, borne aloft
             Or sinking as the light wind lives or dies;
       And full-grown lambs loud bleat from hilly bourn;
          Hedge-crickets sing; and now with treble soft
          The red-breast whistles from a garden-croft;
             And gathering swallows twitter in the skies.

Introduction

Other poems for nature might include the extract from Wordsworth's 'The Prelude' and Heaney's 'Death of a Naturalist', but for an alternative perspective consider how Rita Dove uses the hurricane as a starting point to think about relationships in 'Cozy Apologia' or how Rupert Brooke's 'The Soldier' explores the rich bounty of England as a method of expressing his patriotism. Remember, diligent exploration of different themes and connections is one of the most rewarding and productive methods of revision – it's much more effective than just learning quotations!

"In both Dickinson's 'As Imperceptibly as Grief' and John Keats's 'To Autumn', nature is personified as an entity that reminds the poets of their own mortality. In focusing also on the themes of change and beauty, these poems make clear how versatile[3] and impactful nature can be as a poetic topic and frame for writers to explore their own lives."

Theme/Paragraph One: For both writers, nature offers a way of poignantly exploring mortality and grief.

- The focus in 'To Autumn' on mortality is unsurprising: Keats had recognised his symptoms of tuberculosis in 1819-20, a disease he was intimately familiar with having cared for his mother who died of the same disease when the poet was just 14 years old, and 'To Autumn' was one of his last poems. Keats then died in 1821. With this context in mind, 'To Autumn' becomes an intensely personal reflection on death and dying, which is seen in part in the apostrophe of the poem's title. In directing the poem 'To' Autumn, there is an added respect and reverence for this period of change, which is also highlighted through the increasing tone of contemplation that comes through Keats's use of rhetorical questions that open the second and third stanzas. As 'To Autumn' continues, then, Keats seems to be intimately questioning his own life at this vital period. [*AO2 for close analysis of the author's use of form, structure and language. AO3 for demonstrating an understanding of how the context shapes the text*].

- <u>Pivot to comparison:</u> Dickinson is now famously known for her seclusion from her twenties throughout the rest of her life. She was a recluse and throughout her writing there is a focus on the incoming darkness and potential brevity of happiness. These traits are seen in 'As Imperceptibly as Grief', which is both an elegy for summer and a metaphor for Dickinson's fear of death. At the beginning of the poem, she writes that summer has 'lapsed away' – the word 'lapsed' has a gentle quality. This sense of loss being non-invasive is also seen through the use of polyptoton ('imperceptibly' and 'imperceptible'), which stresses how slight and subtle this grief is. In focusing on the end of summer, however, Dickinson stresses the way in which grief too will go with time. [*AO1 for incorporating textual references to justify and support an interpretation. AO2 for close analysis of the author's use of language. AO3 for demonstrating an understanding of how the context shapes the text*].

- In a similar way, Dickinson uses rhyme to note the way in which her grief is changing. The ABCB scheme allows for points of connection and resonance whilst also allowing for moments where her ideas stand alone (on the A and C lines and often on the slant rhymes).[4] In doing so, Dickinson acknowledges how this is a period of uncertainty, almost disconnection. [*AO2 for close analysis of the author's use of form*].

Theme/Paragraph Two: Nature therefore becomes an effective way of considering how change can impact an individual.

- Change is written into the very structure of Keats's 'To Autumn'. At the beginning of each stanza he uses an ABAB rhyme scheme; however, this is then replaced by a looser CDEDCCE scheme. In using this variation, Keats demonstrates how the Autumnal period is one predominantly of change, although he leaves it somewhat ambiguous if this is good or bad. At the end of the first stanza, for example, while focusing on the bees, it is observed that 'they think warm days will never cease, / For Summer has o'erbrimm'd their clammy cells.' The emphasis on the word 'think' adds a surprising note to the first stanza, which is mostly about the beauty of Autumn – now, it is as if nature deceives the bees, with the notion of their 'clammy cells' also having some connotations of discomfort or displeasure. [*AO1 for incorporating textual references to justify and support an interpretation. AO2 for close analysis of the author's use of form, structure and language*].
- That Autumn is a time of change is also hinted at through the use of double meanings during the poem's opening lines. Autumn is personified as a 'Close bosom-friend of the maturing sun' – whilst the sun does 'mature' the crops and help them grow, the adjective also notes how the sun is growing older. Keats thus implies how for all of the friendliness of

this time, there's a slightly darker, subtler suggestion of how change is about to come with the passing of the seasons. [*AO2 for close analysis of the author's use of language*].

- <u>Pivot to comparison:</u> It is perhaps ironic that a woman who spent so much time in the same situation should write so movingly about change, and yet Dickinson's 'As Imperceptibly as Grief' is striking in the variety of ways with which it registers how change can affect an individual. There is an intense, quiet tone to the poem that emerges in part in the knowledge of Dickinson's isolation, which would have often led to hours of reflection and contemplation. There are numerous oxymorons throughout the poem that indicate how impactful change (and grief) can be. For example, the 'Morning', a period of hope and renewal, 'foreign shone', with the adverb 'foreign' adding a suggestion of strangeness, perhaps even discomfort, at this change. In the next lines, the Morning is described as having 'A courteous, yet harrowing Grace, / As Guest, that would be gone'. These juxtapositions ('courteous, yet harrowing') and the simile build together into a surprising depiction of Morning as something that is not necessarily welcoming. This moment of change illustrates how nature can become a frame to express feelings that are unexpected – but through this deflation, both writers suggest how effective nature can be as a poetic way of writing about grief. [*AO1 for incorporating textual references to justify and support an interpretation. AO2 for close analysis of the author's use of structure and language. AO3 for demonstrating an understanding of how the context shapes the text*].

Theme/Paragraph Three: Despite this somewhat darker focus in both poems, it is impossible to ignore the beauty that both poets also attach to nature and the changing of the seasons.

- Romantic poetry often explored the power of nature, with Keats's 'To Autumn' being a prime example of how writers from this period idolised the power of the natural world. The suggestion of nature's fertility is captured in the opening stanza of Keats's 'To Autumn' through the use of enjambment – as each line moves into the next, focusing on another part of nature's bounty, it is hard to ignore the sense of nature overbrimming with so much life. This is further emphasised through Keats's use of a lexical field of excess ('swell', 'plump', 'o'erbrimmed'), which captures the richness of nature just before it is about to change. Finally, Keats breaks from the traditional 10 lined stanzas used in odes, instead using 11 lines, a final reminder of how much food there is and how 'bless[ed]' we are to receive it from this generous goddess. [*AO1 for incorporating textual references to justify and support an interpretation. AO2 for close analysis of the author's use of structure and language. AO3 for demonstrating an understanding of how the context shapes the text*].
- Indeed, when Keats personifies Autumn in the second stanza, he chooses to offer not a grand image of a God, but instead something unusual, relaxed and affable. It is a figure who sits 'careless', intoxicated by 'the fume of poppies' and who is occasionally 'like a gleaner', with Keats's simile illustrating how this figure is

happy in poverty (a gleaner was a peasant who relied on the leftovers of a harvest). Similarly, in the third stanza Keats observes 'thou hast thy music too' – Keats's pastoral vision then is imagined in a figure who goes against our expectations of the Gods. In being content with the simpler, more natural things in life, this enigmatic, affable creation illustrates the personable and enjoyable elements of nature's cycle. [AO2 *for close analysis of the author's use of language*].

- <u>Pivot to comparison:</u> Keats focuses on nature's beauty, and similarly at the end of her poem Dickinson presents nature as an almost supernatural force. Nature at the conclusion of the poem ('And thus' implies Dickinson is coming the end of her reflection) becomes an indomitable force that rejects implements for travel (a 'Wing' or 'Keel') and instead 'made her light escape / Into the Beautiful.' At this point, Dickinson no longer uses the dashes that are so common to her style, with the enjambment instead capturing the simple force of this movement, with 'light' adding an ethereal quality to this action. Although transient and unusual, it is difficult not to be taken by how slight and 'imperceptible' this final movement is. [AO2 *for close analysis of the author's use of form and language*].

Conclusion

"Both poems distinctly remind readers then that the transience of nature is what makes it so beautiful – for both Keats and Dickinson, writing about nature at a point of change allows them to explore ideas around grief, mortality, change and beauty. Nature has always given, and will continue to provide, inspiration for poets, for even at the end something new can emerge that is, as per the end of Dickinson's poem, 'Beautiful.'"

An image of John Keats, rapt in thought.

PAIRING IV: POWER
'OZYMANDIAS' & 'HAWK ROOSTING'

Part a: Read Percy Bysshe Shelley's 'Ozymandias'. Shelley's poem is about power. How does Shelley present power in the poem? Remember to refer to the contexts of the poem in your answer. [15 marks]

Ozymandias
Percy Shelley

I met a traveller from an antique land,
Who said—"Two vast and trunkless legs of stone
Stand in the desert. . . . Near them, on the sand,
Half sunk a shattered visage lies, whose frown,
And wrinkled lip, and sneer of cold command,
Tell that its sculptor well those passions read
Which yet survive, stamped on these lifeless things,
The hand that mocked them, and the heart that fed;

And on the pedestal, these words appear:
My name is Ozymandias, King of Kings;
Look on my Works, ye Mighty, and despair!
Nothing beside remains. Round the decay
Of that colossal Wreck, boundless and bare
The lone and level sands stretch far away."

Introduction

I've got a slight contextual reference in this introduction, just to be getting those AO3 marks from the beginning.

> "In 'Ozymandias', Percy Bysshe Shelley reminds readers that human power is temporary; as might be expected from a poem written during the Romantic period, this work reminds readers that nature's power is indomitable."

Theme/Paragraph One: In Shelley's poem, the statue of Ozymandias is supposed to be a symbol of his power and tyrannical rule; however, human power is overall portrayed as fleeting.

- Although only ruins of Ozymandias' statue remain, what details are presented in the poem suggest how grand and imposing the statue once was. Shelley's language implies its size ('vast'); however, this is drawn into sharp contrast with the statue's destroyed state ('colossal Wreck'). Moreover, the head of the

statue captures the figure's tyrannical rule: his 'frown, / And wrinkled lip, and [the] sneer of cold command' all together emphasise how unpleasant Ozymandias was as a ruler. [*AO1 for incorporating textual references to justify and support an interpretation. AO2 for close analysis of the author's use of language*].
- This is consistent with the presentation of the Egyptian Pharaoh elsewhere in Shelley's poetry, which often presented him as a symbol of political tyranny. All that is left of Ozymandias's statue in the poem reminds readers of his cruelty. For example, the statue's epitaph reads 'My name is Ozymandias, King of Kings; / Look on my Works, ye Mighty, and despair!' The imperative ('Look on') and the exclamation together demonstrate how statues are carefully crafted symbols of an individual's power. That individual chooses which persona they want to portray, and for Shelley's Ozymandias he illustrates his arrogance through this statue. [*AO2 for close analysis of the author's use of language. AO3 for demonstrating an understanding of how the context shapes the text*].
- Furthermore, Shelley implies that the sculptor's portrayal of Ozymandias is a form of silent rebellion against the ruler, which also suggests that this 'King of Kings' was not as completely powerful as he might have first thought. There is little love or respect in the observation of how the ruler's likeness is 'stamped on these lifeless things' – both the verb and adjective together are cold and without any respect for the Pharaoh. This symbol of Ozymandias' power, therefore, is not as potent as he might have first thought. [*AO1 for incorporating textual references to*

justify and support an interpretation. AO2 for close analysis of the author's use of language].

Theme/Paragraph Two: Alongside the faded statue, Shelley's poem also explores the constant power of nature and time, which is to be expected from a Romantic poet.

- However, the language that stresses the statue's (former) size is matched by a language of brokenness ('trunkless' and 'shattered') and emptiness ('bare') that demonstrates how human power does not last. After the epitaph, it is observed how 'Nothing beside remains', with Shelley's short sentence deflating the (supposed) expression of power in the epitaph. Shelley's disdain for this weathered statue (and all it represents) is clear. [*AO1 for incorporating textual references to justify and support an interpretation. AO2 for close analysis of the author's use of language*].
- The form of Shelley's sonnet emphasises change. Instead of the regular ABBAABBA CDCDCD scheme of the sonnet (there are, of course, variations in this rhyme scheme), the rhyme scheme of Shelley's sonnet is: ABABACDCDEDEFEF. This focus on change and inconsistency illustrates how nothing is certain other than the passing of time – anything that tries to cement a human's presence on this world (for example, a statue) will fail. [*AO2 for close analysis of the author's use of form. AO3 for demonstrating an understanding of how the context shapes the text*].
- Of course, this should be expected from a Romantic poet – writers from this movement venerated and

respected nature's power. Ozymandias' statue has not been destroyed by other men but by nature. This message is amplified by the poem's mysterious frame: this traveller 'from an antique land' who visits deserts that are made up of 'lone and level sands' that 'stretch far away' tells the narrator ('I met') about their discovery. In this foreign setting, nature is portrayed as being as unforgiving as Ozymandias himself, with the adjective 'decay' towards the end of the poem highlighting how nature's processes have overcome the statue – with time, it shall be buried and forgotten. [*AO2 for close analysis of the author's use of structure and language. AO3 for demonstrating an understanding of how the context shapes the text*].

Conclusion

Another hint of context in this conclusion, just for something extra to say.

> "Shelley wrote 'Ozymandias' after being challenged by a friend, Horace Smith, to write a poem with the Pharaoh's name as the title. The two would then compare their work. This suggestion of human competition and the desire to be remembered offers a clear link to the poem's moral: an individual's success and achievements will be celebrated during their lifetime, but beyond that, nature will always find a way to assert its power."

Part b: Choose one other poem from the anthology in which the poet also writes about power. Compare the way the poet presents power in your chosen poem with the way Percy Bysshe Shelley presents power in 'Ozymandias'. [25 marks]

In your answer you should compare:

• **the content and structure of the poems – what they are about and how they are organised**

• **how the writers create effects, using appropriate terminology where relevant**

• **the contexts of the poems, and how these may have influenced the ideas in them.**

Introduction

"Together, Shelley's 'Ozymandias' and Ted Hughes's 'Hawk Roosting' are about power. But where both poems use an expressive tyrannical voice to explore how power can corrupt an individual, they explore in greater detail how influential and impressive nature can be."

PAIRING IV: POWER

Theme/Paragraph One: Both poems create and explore the voice of a powerful and tyrannical figure.

- Hughes uses the dramatic monologue form to create a narrative voice that is both powerful and tyrannical. Whilst some have read Hughes's hawk as being a representation of the dictators seen during the twentieth century, it has been suggested by the poet himself that the poem is more about the power of nature. Moreover, throughout 'Hawk Roosting', Hughes hints about the hawk's egotism through the constant use of personal pronouns. In particular, the poem begins and ends with statements that begin with 'I' – this frame highlights the hawk's narcissism. [*AO1 for incorporating textual references to justify and support an interpretation. AO2 for close analysis of the author's use of structure and language. AO3 for demonstrating an understanding of how the context shapes the text*].
- From the poem's opening line, Hughes shows the hawk's confidence in noting how it 'sit[s] in the top of the wood' with its 'eyes closed' – this predator, already at the 'top', need not watch out for other hunters. In the next line, Hughes captures the hawk's 'Inaction' by following the word with a caesura, creating a strong break in the line, again emphasising the animal's assurance. When describing itself, the hawk focuses on its 'hooked head and hooked feet', with Hughes' repetition anticipating the animal's later admittance that there is 'no sophistry' in its body. Such is the hawk's power and love of hunting that even when it

sleeps it 'rehearse[s] perfect kills'. In this first stanza, therefore, Hughes introduces this powerful predator by focusing on its confidence and its dedication to death. [AO2 for close analysis of the author's use of language].

- Pivot to comparison: Similarly, Shelley's 'Ozymandias' creates a figure who is likewise arrogant, as seen by the descriptions throughout the poem that emphasise how large the statue once was. The 'legs of stone' are described as 'vast' at the beginning of the poem, whilst at the end of the work the same statue is described as a 'colossal Wreck'. Furthermore, the statue's inscription states: 'My name is Ozymandias, King of Kings; / Look on my Works, ye Mighty, and despair!' Shelley's imperative and exclamation together highlight how this figure imagines the statue to be a statement of his domineering power over the world. [AO1 for incorporating textual references to justify and support an interpretation. AO2 for close analysis of the author's use of language].

Theme/Paragraph Two: However, the two poems explore how power can corrupt an individual.

- One of the ways in which Hughes implies the hawk's narcissism is through the repeated emphasis in the second stanza that the hawk believes nature has been made for it. The hawk talks about 'The convenience of the high trees', how the 'air's buoyancy and the sun's ray / Are of advantage to me'. Suggesting at the end of the stanza that 'the earth's face upward for my inspection', Hughes's use of the verb 'inspection' places the hawk as being in complete control of the

world below it. [*AO2 for close analysis of the author's use of language*].
- Pivot to comparison: Likewise, Shelley's poem explores how easy it is for a figure to be a tyrant. Ramesses II was a Pharaoh in Ancient Egypt for 66 years and in Shelley's poetry he often represents political tyranny. Although the statue's head has become 'shattered', it still has a 'frown, / And wrinkled lip, and [a] sneer of cold command'. These details together imply how all that remains of Ramesses is his cruelty. [*AO2 for close analysis of the author's use of language. AO3 for demonstrating an understanding of how the context shapes the text*].
- Furthermore it is described how arrogant and uncaring Ozymandias was. This statue represented 'The hand that mocked them, and the heart that fed' to the ruler's subjects. Equally, this focus on the abuse of power is ironic, as although the statue suggests how the ruler abused his power, it is stressed that this power is fleeting. Now, the statue is 'stamped' with emotion, but these remaining pieces of the statue are 'lifeless things'. Moreover, the statue is situated in a place that is 'boundless and bare' and 'The lone and level sands stretch far away'. Whilst the statue therefore suggests how power has corrupted Ozymandias, Shelley makes it clear that this power will not last. [*AO1 for incorporating textual references to justify and support an interpretation. AO2 for close analysis of the author's use of language.*].

Theme/Paragraph Three: Shelley's poem explores how human power is temporary, stressing instead how nature will overcome whatever monument an

individual might try to create to celebrate their achievements. Hughes likewise explores the power of nature.

- Whilst Ozymandias uses the statue to symbolise his power, Shelley explores how nature cannot be diminished by suggesting that time and nature are easily stronger than any form of human power, a point that should be unsurprising given Shelley was a Romantic poet (the Romantic writers often write about the power of nature). Shelley adapts the sonnet form of the poem by using an unusual and irregular rhyme scheme (ABABACDCEDEFEF), which illustrates how any attempts to permanently capture a person's power is destined to fail. Furthermore, the 'traveller' describing the statue states 'Nothing beside remains', with Shelley's short sentence deflating the statements and tone of grandeur that Ozymandias is attempting to create when referring to himself. [*AO2 for close analysis of the author's use of form and language*].
- <u>Pivot to comparison:</u> In 'Hawk Roosting', the natural cycle of predators hunting prey is captured in graphic detail. Whilst the violence depicted is to be expected from a hawk, the poem's portrayal of raw, emotionless and unsentimental arrogance is striking and suggests Hughes's familiarity with the natural world (he was born and brought up in Yorkshire). Hughes's hawk observes 'I kill where I please because it is all mine', with the mostly monosyllabic words highlighting the brutal simplicity of the hawk's mentality (which is also seen in the observation that there is 'no sophistry in my body'). Similarly, the hawk notes 'My manners are

tearing off heads' – alongside this graphic language, Hughes's oxymoron (there's little polite about this behaviour) illustrates the brutal element of nature's power. [*AO1 for incorporating textual references to justify and support an interpretation. AO2 for close analysis of the author's use of language*].
- In the final stanza of Hughes's poem, it is repeatedly stressed how the hawk wants to 'keep things like this.' Each line of this final quatrain uses an end-stopped line, which suggests the definitive control and consequent confidence the hawk has at this situation. In a similar vein, Hughes's six quatrain stanza also highlights the regularity of this control: the hawk has its kingdom firmly established, and it wants to maintain this order. The natural world is presented as unapologetically savage. [*AO2 for close analysis of the author's use of structure and form*].

Conclusion

"Power manifests in different forms, but it is important to note that both poems return to the same idea: nature is powerful, threatening and irrepressible. Both poets present tyrannical characters, but Ozymandias's human power is nothing when compared with the ferocity of Hughes's hawk."

Percy Bysshe Shelley.

Percy Shelley was one of the most influential voices of the Romantic movement.

UNSEEN POETRY

PAIRING I: DREAMS

Guidance

Before we jump in to the first poetic pairing on dreams, I want to outline a few practical things you might want to do when you turn the page and begin thinking about the unseen poetry. The first point is simple: don't panic! If you panic, your brain will shut down and you'll struggle to take anything in. When you read the poems, have your pen ready and circle any particular words you like, or identify any techniques that you think might be important. Once you start to note these points, you'll settle into the task, at which point you should read the poems again and make more annotations. *Et voila* – you'll have ideas to write about.

It's important that you engage with and be sensitive to the larger ideas behind the poem – as always, try not to get too bogged down in the technical details. As before, begin by offering an overview of the poem's meaning and then track through the poem for Part 1; for Part 2, you can similarly work through the poems but try to offer some thematic links through your paragraph topics. Regardless, you want to be as thorough with both poems as possible (but make sure you've got two paragraphs of analysis, as paragraphs are important when you write and you don't want to hit your examiner with a wall of written text).

Use these exemplar answers as a way of preparing for your own exam – before reading my answers, annotate the poems yourself and decide what are the key themes and messages from the poems. You may well disagree with my readings and paragraph topics, but that's fine – every answer to unseen poetry should deserve credit if it's based on the text!

Read the two poems, 'About My Dreams' by Hilda Conkling and 'As I Grew Older' by Langston Hughes. In both of these poems the poets write about dreams.

Write about the poem 'About my Dreams' by Hilda Conkling, and its effect on you. [15 marks]

You may wish to consider:

• what the poem is about and how it is organised

• the ideas the poet may have wanted us to think about

• the poet's choice of words, phrases and images and the effects they create

• how you respond to the poem.

'About My Dreams'
By Hilda Conkling

Now the flowers are all folded
And the dark is going by.
The evening is arising . . .
It is time to rest.
When I am sleeping
I find my pillow full of dreams.
They are all new dreams:
No one told them to me
Before I came through the cloud.
They remember the sky, my little dreams,
They have wings, they are quick, they are sweet.
Help me tell my dreams
To the other children,
So that their bread may taste whiter,
So that the milk they drink
May make them think of meadows
In the sky of stars.
Help me give bread to the other children
So that their dreams may come back:
So they will remember what they knew
Before they came through the cloud.
Let me hold their little hands in the dark,
The lonely children,
The babies that have no mothers any more.
Dear God, let me hold up my silver cup
For them to drink,
And tell them the sweetness
Of my dreams.

Introduction:

> "Hilda Conkling's 'About My Dreams' explores how having a dream can mean so much to those who lack worldly things, with the poem focusing on children and what having a dream can do for them."

Theme/Paragraph One: At the beginning of the poem, Conkling explores the sense of delight that comes with dreams.

- In the first few lines of 'About My Dreams', Conkling establishes an image of an oncoming darkness. The tone of these opening lines is uncertain: whilst the ellipses of 'The evening is arising…' is almost worried, the assured suggestion that 'It is time to rest.' gives an idea of relaxation. This is confirmed in the metaphor that, when Conkling's speaker is sleeping, 'I find my pillow full of dreams' – this metaphor adds a sense of optimism and comfort to these dreams. Furthermore, Conkling personifies her dreams as 'my little dreams, / They have wings, they are quick, they are sweet.' These cute dreams are comforting and relaxing, almost like small Cupids, and provide Conkling's speaker with a sense of joy. [*AO1 for incorporating textual references to justify and support an interpretation. AO2 for close analysis of the author's use of language*].
- The dramatic monologue form of Conkling's poem allows the writer to create an intensely personal

account of what it is like to have dreams and the potential to share them with other people. At one point, the speaker asks an unnamed individual to 'Help me tell my dreams / To the other children'. Dreams will help 'their bread' 'taste whiter' and their milk will help 'them think of meadows / In the sky of stars.' Conkling suggests dreams offer a form of imaginative escape, with the enjambment highlighting this sense of freedom, whilst the focus on food implies the way in which dreams offer a form of spiritual sustenance[1] for those who have them or who share them. [*AO2 for close analysis of the author's use of form and language*].

Theme/Paragraph Two: It is touching how Conkling's speaker wants to share their dreams with others and to support the children to have dreams of their own.

- Conkling repeats her plea for God to 'Help me' give dreams to children. This repetition adds a tone of almost desperation to this desire, whilst the anaphora of 'So' at the beginning of the coming lines suggests how dreams have various benefits to those who have them. Conkling's speaker hopes that, when the children learn of her dreams, 'their dreams may come back', a stark contrast to the earliest suggestion of darkness at the beginning of the poem. [*AO1 for incorporating textual references to justify and support an interpretation. AO2 for close analysis of the author's use of form and language*].

- Conkling stresses how weak the children are whom she wants to reach with her dreams. The suggestion that she wants to 'hold their little hands in the dark' implies that dreams provide some form of solace to these children, with the adjective 'little' stressing how feeble[2] these young people are. At the end of the poem, Conkley directly addresses God, with the apostrophe implying both the significance and the importance of her invocation and how essential it is that these children receive some form of support. [*AO2 for close analysis of the author's use of language*].

Conclusion

"At the end of the poem, Conkling writes about the 'sweetness / Of my Dreams.' This language of lightness and happiness runs throughout the poem, reminding readers about how dreams are often a positive experience for those who have them."

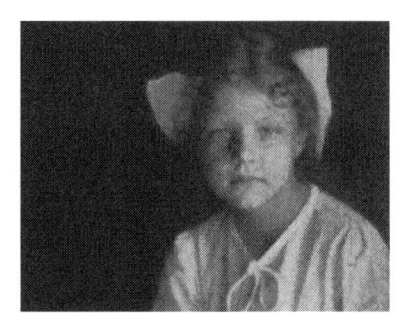

Hilda Conkling wrote many of her poems at an extremely young age!

PAIRING I: DREAMS

Now compare 'As I Grew Older' by Langston Hughes and 'About My Dreams' by Hilda Conkling. [25 marks]

You should compare:

- **what the poems are about and how they are organised**
- **the ideas the poets may have wanted us to think about**
- **the poets' choice of words, phrases and images and the effects they create**
- **how you respond to the poems.**

'As I Grew Older'
By Langston Hughes

It was a long time ago.
I have almost forgotten my dream.
But it was there then,
In front of me,
Bright like a sun,—
My dream.

And then the wall rose,
Rose slowly,
Slowly,
Between me and my dream.
Rose slowly, slowly,
Dimming,

Hiding,
The light of my dream.
Rose until it touched the sky,—
The wall.

Shadow.
I am black.

I lie down in the shadow.
No longer the light of my dream before me,
Above me.
Only the thick wall.
Only the shadow.

My hands!
My dark hands!
Break through the wall!
Find my dream!
Help me to shatter this darkness,
To smash this night,
To break this shadow
Into a thousand lights of sun,
Into a thousand whirling dreams
Of sun!

Introduction

"Both poems by Conkling and Langston Hughes are about dreams and they suggest how they can push against inequalities. Where Hughes's poem is about the difficulties he faces as a black man, Conkling explores how dreams can help the poorest in society."

Theme/Paragraph One: For both poets, dreams represent hope and optimism that the world might be a better place.

- The use of anaphora throughout Hughes's poem ('I' and 'My') frames the poem as an intensely personal response to the writer's personal situation and the challenges he seemed to face throughout his life. Hughes's poem explores the experiences of a black man in a world that appears to be hostile towards him; the end-stopped, short sentence 'I am black' is as much a statement as it is a declaration of the challenges that he faces. This line comes in a two-lined stanza, with the line before simply stating 'Shadow' – the darkness of the speaker's skin is matched by the darkness cast by the imposing wall. [*AO1 for incorporating textual references to justify and support an interpretation. AO2 for close analysis of the author's use of form and language*].
- <u>Pivot to comparison:</u> As might be expected, both poets use a language of light to describe their dreams. In the opening stanza of his poem, Hughes describes his dream as 'Bright like a sun', with the simile adding connotations of warmth, light and happiness to this dream. Conkling's poem opens by introducing an image of darkness ('Now the flowers are folded / And the dark is going by.'), but her dreams provide solace, as suggested through the metaphor 'I find my pillow full of dreams'. [*AO1 for incorporating textual*

references to justify and support an interpretation. AO2 for close analysis of the author's use of language].

- Conkling's dreams are personified as cute, like small Cupids: 'my little dreams, / They have wings, they are quick, they are sweet.' This language illustrates the inherent optimism that comes with having dreams, and Conkling's speaker then states that she needs support to 'tell my dreams / To the other children'. These dreams seem to encourage and support these children: 'So that their bread may taste whiter' and it will transform the milk to 'make them think of meadows.' This rural idyll symbolises peace and tranquillity, with Conkling's focus on food suggesting how dreams offer a form of almost spiritual sustenance to those who have them. [*AO2 for close analysis of the author's use of language*].

Theme/Paragraph Two: But where Conkling talks about her dreams in the present tense, Hughes writes about his dreams as things that have now gone.

- Conkling's poem is a dramatic monologue, which adds a sense of immediacy to its sentiments. As part of this, the speaker's dreams are alive and fresh: 'They are all new dreams: / No one told them to me'. These 'new' dreams are accompanied with a desire to use them to support 'The lonely children', with the point 'Let me hold their little hands in the dark' suggesting how Conkling wants to use her dreams to support others. Conkling's present tense pleas to God ('Help me') illustrate how important it is for everyone to have

dreams and the good they can do. [*AO1 for incorporating textual references to justify and support an interpretation. AO2 for close analysis of the author's use of form and language*].
- Pivot to comparison: But where Conkling seems to suggest her dreams offer her a form of respite[3] from a world that is symbolically dark ('the dark is going by'), Hughes focuses on the wall that has gone up between him and his dreams. Hughes uses an extended metaphor throughout the poem to explore how a 'wall rose [...] Between me and my dream.' This wall symbolises the difficulties that Hughes faced throughout his life. It is a wall that, according to Hughes, 'Rose slowly, / Slowly', a point that is repeated ('Rose slowly, slowly') – the repetition and frequent caesuras together represent the difficulties that have risen against Hughes. [*AO1 for incorporating textual references to justify and support an interpretation. AO2 for close analysis of the author's use of language*].
- And yet, Hughes suggests there might be some hope as at the end of the poem he realises the potential power of his 'dark hands', which he will use to 'Break through the wall! / Find my dream!' The use of four exclamation marks and the imperative suggests how Hughes hungers to break down the wall in front of him. The language of destruction in this final stanza ('shatter', 'smash' and 'break') however is mostly metaphorical ('smash this night'), which highlights how the barriers Hughes faces are not literal but ideological[4] – that is, they are focused around race and identity – and how he is determined to challenge them. This opportunity to free his dream clearly

excites Hughes, as the enjambment in this final stanza is a stark contrast to the short, one-line sentences that have been used throughout the poem. This difference in sentence length demonstrates how when he thinks of breaking down the wall, Hughes becomes optimistic and delighted at the thought of freeing his dream. [*AO1 for incorporating textual references to justify and support an interpretation. AO2 for close analysis of the author's use of form, structure and language*].

Conclusion

> "Dreams are important for society, whether that be to address racial inequalities as in Hughes or apparent poverty and social inequalities as in Conkling. Conkling has a language of lightness and happiness throughout her poem that characterises dreams as being solely positive entities: addressing God at the end of the poem, she hopes the children will learn of 'the sweetness / Of my dreams.' Dreams should always be sweet, but as Hughes shows, it is very easy for them to become sour."

A portrait of Langston Hughes by the artist Winold Reiss.

PAIRING II: LOSS/SADNESS/ISOLATION

Guidance

Thankfully, the assessment objectives used to mark your answers to the Unseen Poetry section are the same as those used in the Poetry Anthology section. AO1 (which is, you'll remember, **both** the way you write and the way you use evidence (quotations or details) to support your points) and AO2 (your ability to analyse language, form and structure).

But although this time you don't need contextual material (yay!), you **do** need to ensure you're making comparisons between both texts. This does not have a separate assessment objective, but is examined across both AO1 and AO2 – at the top of the mark band, your comparisons will be 'critical, illuminating and sustained'. Remember that one way of achieving this is ensuring your paragraphs are structured around comparisons – using the thematic method means your analysis of techniques fits nicely under an umbrella and you can't just be accused of feature spotting (when you mindlessly list the various techniques in the poem).

Many of the same ideas that were discussed in the first section apply again to this section: make it clear to your examiner that you fully understand the poems; state clearly where in the poem you're analysing, to help keep your examiner rooted and clear about your analysis; poetic terminology should only enhance an answer, and you need to focus on the effect of the techniques to get those AO2 marks. Feature spotting remains a bad thing to do and should be avoided. Keep your sentences and quotations short to ensure your work is easy to follow and use signposting terms to make it clear to your examiner when you are comparing the two poems.

Read the two poems, 'The Voice' by Thomas Hardy and 'Loneliness' by Katherine Mansfield. In both of these poems the poets write about isolated individuals.

Write about the poem 'The Voice' by Thomas Hardy, and its effect on you. [15 marks]

You may wish to consider:

• what the poem is about and how it is organised

• the ideas the poet may have wanted us to think about

• the poet's choice of words, phrases and images and the effects they create

• how you respond to the poem.

'The Voice'
Thomas Hardy

Woman much missed, how you call to me, call to me,
Saying that now you are not as you were
When you had changed from the one who was all
    to me,
But as at first, when our day was fair.

Can it be you that I hear? Let me view you, then,
Standing as when I drew near to the town
Where you would wait for me: yes, as I knew you then,
Even to the original air-blue gown!

Or is it only the breeze, in its listlessness*
Travelling across the wet mead to me here,
You being ever consigned to existlessness,*
Heard no more again far or near?

Thus I; faltering forward,
Leaves around me falling,
Wind oozing thin through the thorn from norward*
And the woman calling.

* **Listlessness means** having a lack of energy.
* **Existlessness** suggests living in a state of pale inattentiveness.
* **Norward** means the north.

Introduction

> "Hardy's 'The Voice' is clearly about losing a loved one. The intimate way in which Hardy writes about his 'Woman much missed' suggests this is an autobiographical poem, which goes some way to explain its intense tone of anguish throughout."

Theme/Paragraph One: From the beginning of the poem, Hardy is questioning whether or not he can actually hear his loved one 'call to [him]'.

- Hardy's poem opens with the repetition of 'call to me' – this creates an unusual echo to the poem that establishes the one-sided relationship between Hardy's speaker and the ghost, with the former trying to work out who (or what) the latter is. In the second stanza, Hardy tries to assert some form of control over the ghost, asking first 'Can it be you that I hear?' before commanding it: 'Let me view you'. Hardy wishes to view this 'Woman' as they were when they were younger, with the woman wearing 'the original air-blue gown'. [*AO1 for incorporating textual references to justify and support an interpretation. AO2 for close analysis of the author's use of language*].
- Throughout Hardy's poem the word 'you' is repeated, which continuously stresses how much Hardy misses this figure and creates a tone of longing within the poem. This is also seen through Hardy's use of enjambment, which imbues the poem with the

suggestion that Hardy is searching for the answers. This is seen in the third stanza, for example, which is one extended question as Hardy tries to understand whether it is only the sounds of nature that are confusing him and not the voice of his deceased partner. [AO2 for close analysis of the author's use of form and language].

Theme/Paragraph Two: Hardy's poem shows how the world around him has become grey and lifeless now that this woman has gone.

- When in the third stanza Hardy turns to nature as a potential cause for his hallucination, it is noted how the breeze has a quality of 'listlessness' about it. This personification casts nature as aimless and empty, with no direction – this use of pathetic fallacy perfectly mirrors Hardy's speaker's own lethargy[1] and sense of inaction. Moreover, the word 'listlessness' is rhymed with 'existlessness' – both overlong words stress the woman's nonexistence and the emptiness that Hardy's speaker now must live with. [AO1 for incorporating textual references to justify and support an interpretation. AO2 for close analysis of the author's use of form and language].
- It is unsurprising, then, that in the final stanza nature is described as also symbolically dying: the 'Leaves around me [are] falling'. Moreover, the wind is 'oozing thin through the thorn' – whilst the word 'oozing' stresses how thick and unpleasant it has become to live in the world, the word 'thorn' also carries connotations of pain. This is also seen in the opening line of the final stanza: 'Thus I; faltering forward'.

Hardy's caesuras add a stilted pace to the line, capturing how the speaker himself is 'faltering', which is suggestive of the multitude of challenges that he faces now that his loved one is gone. [*AO2 for close analysis of the author's use of form and language*].

Conclusion

"Hardy's 'The Voice' has a profound sense of loss and sadness at its core, and its focus on 'the woman calling' at the poem's beginning and end suggests how, when we lose someone dear, we are desperate to hear them just one more time."

A statue of Thomas Hardy in his home town of Dorchester, UK.

PAIRING II: LOSS/SADNESS/ISOLATION

Now compare 'Loneliness' by Katherine Mansfield and 'The Voice' by Thomas Hardy. [25 marks]

You should compare:

- **what the poems are about and how they are organised**

- **the ideas the poets may have wanted us to think about**

- **the poets' choice of words, phrases and images and the effects they create**

- **how you respond to the poems.**

'Loneliness'
By Katherine Mansfield

Now it is Loneliness who comes at night
Instead of Sleep, to sit beside my bed.
Like a tired child I lie and wait her tread,
I watch her softly blowing out the light.
Motionless sitting, neither left nor right
She turns, and weary, weary droops her head.
She, too, is old; she, too, has fought the fight.
So, with the laurel* she is garlanded.

Through the sad dark the slowly ebbing tide
Breaks on a barren shore, unsatisfied.
A strange wind flows ... then silence. I am fain
To turn to Loneliness, to take her hand,

Cling to her, waiting, till the barren land
Fills with the dreadful monotone of rain.

***Laurel** is a sort of green crown of leaves, often given to the victors of sporting or artistic events.

Introduction

"Both Hardy's 'The Voice' and Katherine Mansfield's 'Loneliness' use a ghostly presence to explore feelings of grief, loss and isolation. There is a deep tone of sadness in both poems, which also use nature as a way of expressing their feelings."

Theme/Paragraph One: In both poems there is a distinct feeling of grief and gloom.

- Mansfield personifies 'Loneliness' from the beginning of the poem. Mansfield refers to this unsettling figure with a mixed tone – there are some maternal elements to her (she comes to 'sit beside my bed') but she is also uncanny, almost supernatural, and is 'Motionless sitting' on the bed. There is something empty about Mansfield's Loneliness, which is emphasised by Mansfield's use of adverbs: 'softly', 'Motionless' and 'weary' in the first stanza together illustrate how Mansfield's Loneliness is quiet and solitary – it is an entity from whom flows a feeling of sadness. [*AO1 for incorporating textual references to justify and support an interpretation. AO2 for close analysis of the author's use of language].*

- However, it is not just Mansfield's Loneliness who is presented with a feeling of sadness. The speaker is 'Like a tired child' who is waiting for loneliness to come, with Mansfield's simile suggesting how the speaker is both innocent and weak. Mansfield's speaker also relates to this figure of the Loneliness, with the parenthetical 'too' towards the end of the first stanza suggesting that the speaker finds some points of connection with her spectral guest. Indeed, in the second stanza the speaker states how she 'Cling[s]' to Loneliness, which has connotations of desperation. *[AO2 for close analysis of the author's use of language].*

- <u>Pivot to comparison:</u> Hardy also uses a ghostly visitor in 'The Voice', but the personal relationship is seen in the strong sense of questioning throughout the poem. The frequent repetition of 'you' throughout all four quatrains adds a sense of longing to the poem, whilst the present tense and rhetorical question of 'Can it be you that I hear?' in the second stanza suggests how Hardy's experience of loss remains an ongoing problem. Moreover, the strategic use of enjambment throughout the poem adds a sense of searching to the work – Hardy's speaker is trying to work through his grief and to understand whose voice it was he heard calling to him. *[AO1 for incorporating textual references to justify and support an interpretation. AO2 for close analysis of the author's use of form and language].*

Theme/Paragraph Two: Both writers also turn to nature as a form of expressing their sadness.

- Mansfield's sonnet first depicts loneliness in the octave before moving more towards nature in the sestet. Throughout the sestet, Mansfield personifies nature as well (the sea is 'unsatisfied') and uses pathetic fallacy to suggest how the internal feelings of sadness also affect how the speaker views the world around her. The language used to describe the rolling waves focuses on its weakness ('slowly ebbing'), as if it has lost its power, whilst the suggestion of the 'barren shore' and the 'barren land' emphasises how this world is no longer alive for Mansfield's speaker (a point that is also captured through the intense repetition of 'barren' in the sestet). Moreover, there is something uncanny in the line 'A strange wind flows… then silence.', with the ellipses and caesura allowing a pause for the reader to contemplate how empty and unusual the world can become when one is isolated. [*AO1 for incorporating textual references to justify and support an interpretation. AO2 for close analysis of the author's use of form, structure and language*].
- <u>Pivot to comparison:</u> The world of Hardy's 'The Voice' has similarly become grey and lifeless. Only when looking into the past does he remember the 'original air-blue gown' – the specificity with which Hardy refers to the colour of the dress suggests how vivid and energised his memory of the past is. Instead, as Hardy thinks about what the cause behind this voice might be, he questions in the third quatrain if it is 'only the breeze', which is 'in its listlessness / Travelling' to him, that causes the noise. Indeed, in

the final stanza Hardy describes how 'Leaves around me [are] falling, / Wind oozing thin' – nature is likewise dying, which is symbolic of Hardy's speaker who thinks increasingly about his own death and the death of his loved one. [*AO1 for incorporating textual references to justify and support an interpretation. AO2 for close analysis of the author's use of language*].
- This suggestion of the grey world around Hardy's speaker is represented also in the poem's structure – the four quintains are set, with little variation or excitement. The world has become marked by its blandness. At the beginning of the final stanza, Hardy's speaker notes how he is 'faltering forward' – the caesuras that come before and after these words add a stilted quality to the poem, with the alliteration carried forward into the next line with the word 'falling'. Hardy's speaker is struggling to continue in this grey world. [*AO2 for close analysis of the author's use of form and structure*].

Conclusion

"Hardy's 'The Voice' begins and ends with the speaker's 'Woman much missed' 'calling' to him. Grief and isolation never go away, and whilst Mansfield's speaker seems to find some solace in her personified Loneliness, for Hardy's speaker to be alone is crippling. Together, these poems remind readers to treasure those nearest to us as they often keep the darkness at bay."

PAIRING III: LONDON

GUIDANCE

Make sure you spend time just reading the poems before you begin writing. Spending five vital minutes just reading and thinking will not be wasted – you've got an hour for the entire section, and should spend roughly twenty minutes on the first question and then the remaining forty minutes on the other. How you split the reading time between the two questions is largely up to you, but just remember the Part 1 question is worth fifteen marks and the Part 2 question is worth twenty-five marks. It's therefore expected that your answer for Part 2 is longer and more in-depth, so make sure you've left plenty of time for it (and generally get your timings right for the entire exam: this is the third section of Paper 2, and it's often reported in Examiner's Reports that there's a feeling that some students have not left enough time for these questions).

Also, pay attention to the introductory blurb. It'll give you a broad statement that helps to guide your initial reading; it's always noted that some students miss this information, which leads to incorrect and misinformed interpretations. Also be aware of 'over-reading', where candidates apply somewhat unusual readings of poems that don't quite make sense. Remember, focus on the details and use quotations to support your point; if there's a point that you can't quite back up using a quotation or detail, then consider whether you should make it.

Finally, try to be as objective and distant from the work as possible; in other words, don't state that you hate the poem or think that it's rubbish. All this will do is make you look naïve – just pretend you're indifferent to the poems and moan about them after the exams to your friends.

Read the two poems, 'A London Thoroughfare. 2 A.M.' by Amy Lowell and 'London grows sad at evening' by Iris Tree. In both of these poems the poets write about London.

Write about the poem 'A London Thoroughfare. 2 A.M.' by Amy Lowell, and its effect on you. [15 marks]

You may wish to consider:

• **what the poem is about and how it is organised**

• **the ideas the poet may have wanted us to think about**

• **the poet's choice of words, phrases and images and the effects they create**

• **how you respond to the poem.**

'A London Thoroughfare. 2 A.M.'
By Amy Lowell

They have watered the street,
It shines in the glare of lamps,
Cold, white lamps,
And lies
Like a slow-moving river,
Barred with silver and black.
Cabs go down it,
One,
And then another.
Between them I hear the shuffling of feet.
Tramps doze on the window-ledges,
Night-walkers pass along the sidewalks.
The city is squalid and sinister,
With the silver-barred street in the midst,
Slow-moving,
A river leading nowhere.

Opposite my window,
The moon cuts,
Clear and round,
Through the plum-coloured night.
She cannot light the city;
It is too bright.
It has white lamps,
And glitters coldly.

I stand in the window and watch the moon.
She is thin and lustreless,

But I love her.
I know the moon,
And this is an alien city.

Introduction

> "Amy Lowell's 'A London Thoroughfare. 2 A.M.' presents a rather dour[1] image of the city. At this quiet hour, Lowell's speaker is struck by the emptiness of the city, which prompts a tone of isolation and loneliness throughout much of the poem."

Theme/Paragraph One: In the first stanza, Lowell portrays London negatively by focusing on the rain and the dirty people around the speaker.

- From the beginning of the poem, Lowell suggests how the light reflected in the wet streets is almost oppressive: 'glare', 'Cold, white' all together suggest that there is little that is positive to be found in this wet city. Indeed, the water on the street is described 'Like a slow-moving river'. Lowell's simile and the use of the enjambment together emphasise how this water is uncontrolled, slowly lolling through the street's gutter. Cabs are said to 'go down' this 'river', but the stark, one-word line of 'One' suggests how empty and quiet the city is. However, there is nothing that is comforting about this description – this is a London that is eerily quiet, marked only by the sounds of the running water. [*AO1 for incorporating textual references to justify and support an interpretation. AO2 for close analysis of the author's use of form, structure and language].*

- With the negative tone of the poem established, Lowell then moves on to describe the people living in the city during the rest of the first stanza. The speaker observes 'I hear the shuffling of feet', with the verb 'shuffling' suggesting how slow and almost pitiful these people are. Alongside 'Tramps', there are 'Night-walkers', which may be a euphemism for prostitutes, all of which leads Lowell's speaker to state that the 'The city is squalid and sinister'. Returning to the river simile from the beginning of the poem, Lowell's speaker concludes at the end of the first stanza that it is 'A river leading nowhere.' This return to the same, depressing trope highlights how London is not an exciting or energising topic for Lowell's speaker, who is left feeling utterly underwhelmed by the world she is observing. [*AO2 for close analysis of the author's use of language*].

Theme/Paragraph Two: Against this gloom, Lowell cannot even find solace in the moon.

- In the second stanza, Lowell introduces the moon, a figure that 'cuts 'Through the plum-coloured night' – however, whilst there is something celebratory and righteous about the verb 'cuts', this is a figure who still 'cannot light the city'. The city remains an inhospitable place – the contradiction 'It is too bright' adds a tone of hostility to the space, where nothing fresh can enter, whilst much of the language in this stanza is not comforting ('bright' and 'white'). The

final line of the stanza describes how this light 'glitters coldly', which has a mixed, almost contradictory tone: the light and positive 'glitters' is contrasted with the negative 'cold'. Lowell therefore stresses how this space, even if lit from above, in unpleasant to be in. [*AO1 for incorporating textual references to justify and support an interpretation. AO2 for close analysis of the author's use of form, structure and language*].
- This attitude continues into the final stanza, in which the moon is personified as being 'thin and lustreless', which highlights how weak the moon is. The poem's consistent focus on how uncomfortable the speaker finds London culminates in the poem's final line: 'And this is an alien city'. The adjective 'alien' suggests how unfamiliar it is for the speaker. This sense of London being an unknown space is also represented in Lowell's use of irregular stanza lengths, which captures how London is 'alien' and indefinable. [*AO1 for incorporating textual references to justify and support an interpretation. AO2 for close analysis of the author's use of form and language*].

Conclusion

"Cities can be overwhelming, but it is rare to see one quiet. However, if Lowell's poem is anything to go by, it is not necessarily a positive experience, as the London seen in this poem is one of disappointment and dejection."

Now compare 'A London Thoroughfare. 2 A. M.' by Amy Lowell and 'London grows sad at evening' by Iris Tree. [25 marks]

You should compare:

• **what the poems are about and how they are organised**

• **the ideas the poets may have wanted us to think about**

• **the poets' choice of words, phrases and images and the effects they create**

• **how you respond to the poems.**

'London grows sad at evening'
By Iris Tree

London grows sad at evening,
And we at the windows sit
To watch her moods,
Wearying with her.
Even a noise of laughter from the street
Sounds in our ears
Like something dropped and shattered on the stone.
Then her musician comes,
A wandering, malicious spirit;
The organ grinder, playing those old tunes
We know too well,
That hurt us with fatigue.
Till Hope like a harlequin,

His glitter hidden in a ragged coat,
The lamplighter, goes by,
Planting his pale flames in the dusk.

Introduction

> "Lowell's 'A London Thoroughfare. 2 A.M.' and Iris Tree's 'London grows sad at evening' share the same frame – the speakers of both poems are looking outside their window and describe the city not as a bustling metropolis but as a quiet and empty space."

Theme/Paragraph One: Both poems focus on how the darkness transforms the city of London.

- At the beginning of Tree's poem, she personifies London as being 'sad' and weary as the darkness comes. The establishes a sombre tone that is maintained through the poem. Indeed, the coming of darkness changes the speaker's worldview completely: laughter becomes 'Like something dropped and shattered on the stone' of the pavements. The simile emphasises how the suggestion of happiness has become painful for the writer, whose morose[2] observations are taken as being typical of the other inhabitants of London who are still awake at this point (the 'we' referenced in the second line). [*AO1 for incorporating textual references to justify and support an interpretation. AO2 for close analysis of the author's use of language*].
- Tree uses the dramatic monologue form to create an

intensely personal poem. It captures the human sadness that comes with darkness and how hopeless a person can feel as the world around them darkens. The poem moves between an iambic and trochaic metre[3], with no consistent rhyme scheme or line length, which illustrates how this nocturnal[4] space has little boundaries or rules. [*AO2 for close analysis of the author's use of form*].

- Pivot to comparison: Lowell's poem similarly depicts London as a space of darkness and confusion. Lowell's alienated speaker focuses on London's inhabitants, describing their 'shuffling of feet' (the word 'shuffling' carries connotations of slowness and almost weakness). Also described are the tramps who 'doze on the window-ledges' and 'Night-walkers', who 'pass along the sidewalks'. Lowell's vague language may hide the fact that these 'Night-walkers' are prostitutes, in which case the euphemism implies that the speaker is trying to give some dignity to the space that she is observing. Nonetheless, this is a city that is 'squalid and sinister', with Lowell's use of irregular stanza lengths amplifying how unordered and unusual the space is. [*AO1 for incorporating textual references to justify and support an interpretation. AO2 for close analysis of the author's use of structure and language*].

Theme/Paragraph Two: Whilst light is introduced in both poems, these poets have different tones when writing about this new entity.

- Tree sets London's darkness against the potential for light represented through the figure of the lamplighter. Darkness ('her musician') is a 'wandering, malicious spirit', who 'hurt[s] us with fatigue' – the adjective 'malicious' suggests how darkness is wicked and evil, and this personified figure of darkness is set directly in opposition to Hope, who, 'like a harlequin', has 'glitter hidden in a ragged coat'. The simile suggests how hope is bright and entertaining, a contrast to the weary dark London, and there is something magical about the description of how the lamplighter brings light with his 'glitter'. In the poem's last line, Tree uses a metaphor, describing how the lamplighter is 'planting his pale flames in the dusk', which allows some final optimism when describing the coming of light, ending the poem on a positive note. [*AO1 for incorporating textual references to justify and support an interpretation. AO2 for close analysis of the author's use of language*].

- <u>Pivot to comparison:</u> This focus on light as representing Hope in Tree's poem offers a contrast with Lowell's poem, which laments that the moon 'cannot light the city'. In Lowell, the moon is personified as being 'thin and lustreless', which suggests an image of weakness and meekness amidst the force of darkness within the city. What language of light there is in Lowell is more about how it is not comforting: 'It is too bright. / It has white lamps'. This harsh light, which is also described at the beginning of the poem as a 'glare', provides little solace to the speaker, but she still 'love[s]' the moon for its familiarity. The city, by contrast, is described as being 'alien', further highlighting the loneliness the speaker feels. [*AO1 for incorporating textual references to justify and support an interpretation. AO2 for close analysis of the author's use of language].*

Conclusion

"Both poems use the word 'glitter', but where in Tree there is some optimism that this 'glitter' brings light (and warmth and 'Hope'), in Lowell the light 'glitters coldly'. The mixed tone is very much indicative of how London is portrayed in both poems: it is a confusing city in which darkness reigns and there is little enjoyment to be had."

Amy Lowell on the cover of Time magazine!

PAIRING IV: BOOKS AND READING

GUIDANCE

At the end of the introduction to this book, I stated the importance of reading, and so it seems fitting at the end of this new study guide to return to the same topic with this final poetry pairing. As both these poems show, reading should and can be a pure delight – it's work that doesn't feel like work, it transforms your perspectives, transports you to new locations (and, sometimes, worlds) and lets you experience events and even emotions that might be unfamiliar. As Guest suggests, books are friends and they'll stick with you – so put down your phone, grab a cuppa and settle down with a good book (after you've finished reading this final set of answers, of course).

Read the two poems, 'Good Books' by Edgar Albert Guest and 'In a Library' by Emily Dickinson. In both of these poems the poets write about reading.

Write about the poem 'Good Books' by Edgar Albert Guest, and its effect on you. [15 marks]

You may wish to consider:

• what the poem is about and how it is organised

• the ideas the poet may have wanted us to think about

• the poet's choice of words, phrases and images and the effects they create

• how you respond to the poem.

'Good Books'
By Edgar Albert Guest

Good books are friendly things to own.
If you are busy they will wait.
They will not call you on the phone
Or wake you if the hour is late.
They stand together row by row,
Upon the low shelf or the high.
But if you're lonesome this you know:
You have a friend or two nearby.

The fellowship of books is real.
They're never noisy when you're still.
They won't disturb you at your meal.
They'll comfort you when you are ill.
The lonesome hours they'll always share.

When slighted they will not complain.
And though for them you've ceased to care
Your constant friends they'll still remain.

Good books your faults will never see
Or tell about them round the town.
If you would have their company
You merely have to take them down.
They'll help you pass the time away,
They'll counsel give if that you need.
He has true friends for night and day
Who has a few good books to read.

Introduction

"In Guest's 'Good Books', he explores the comfort that comes from reading, reminding readers how familiar and relaxing reading can be."

Theme/Paragraph One: In the first stanza, Guest characterises books as 'friendly things to own' by giving them affable[1] personalities.

- From the beginning of the poem, Guest personifies the books. As individuals, these books have multiple human qualities that make them firm friends: they are calm, comforting, patient, respectful and affectionate. At the end of the first stanza, Guest returns to the opening declaration that books are 'friendly', explaining that, 'if you're lonesome', 'You have a

friend or two nearby' in books. This reiterates how congenial[2] books are for those who read them. [*AO1 for incorporating textual references to justify and support an interpretation. AO2 for close analysis of the author's use of language*].
- Indeed, one of the defining qualities of books according to Guest's poem is their constancy – they will be there as needed to support you. This reliability is also seen in the poem's structure – three eight-lined stanzas – that in its regularity amplifies this fidelity.[3] Alongside this, Guest uses an ABAB rhyme scheme to give the poem a light tone. The poem's structure is therefore regular and constant, just like the books it describes. [*AO2 for close analysis of the author's use of form and structure*].

Theme/Paragraph Two: As the poem continues, Guest continues to build upon his characterisation of the books and cumulatively stresses how beneficial they are for those who read.

- In the second stanza, Guest uses a series of end-stopped lines (for example, 'They're never noisy when you're still.'). The impression throughout the second stanza is a never-ending list of the benefits of books. Indeed, the first line of the stanza reads 'The fellowship of books is real', with the term 'fellowship' adding the suggestion that books provide a sense of community and companionship. The constant characterisation of books as positive entities is also seen through the anaphora of 'They' in various forms ('They're' or 'They'll' also included), which focuses the poem exactly on these human-like books that offer a multitude of benefits. [*AO1 for incorporating textual references to justify and support an interpretation. AO2 for close analysis of the author's use of form and language*].

- Indeed, Guest uses enjambment at the end of the second stanza to turn a negative sentiment into a positive one: 'And though for them you've ceased to care / Your constant friends they'll still remain.' Although the first line ends with the sentiment that we might sometimes leave books behind, Guest changes focus in the next line by suggesting how, even then, books will still be 'constant friends', again returning to the 'friendly' quality of books, with the adjective 'constant' implying their dedication. Indeed, this 'constant' reminder of the positive qualities of books is seen again in the third stanza, which begins the same way as at the beginning of the poem with the words 'Good books'. This structural device allows Guest to remind readers time and again of how many benefits there are when reading. [*AO2 for close analysis of the author's use of form, structure and language*].

Conclusion

"Guest rightly never lets readers of his poem forget how beneficial 'Good books' can be. They offer solace when we are sad and are 'constant friends' through thick and thin. As Guest explains at the end of the poem: 'He has true friends for night and day / Who has a few good books to read.'"

Edgar Albert Guest in 1935, reading his poetry over the radio.

PAIRING IV: BOOKS AND READING

Now compare 'Good Books by Edgar Albert Guest and 'In a Library' by Emily Dickinson. [25 marks]

You should compare:

- **what the poems are about and how they are organised**
- **the ideas the poets may have wanted us to think about**
- **the poets' choice of words, phrases and images and the effects they create**
- **how you respond to the poems.**

'In a Library'
By Emily Dickinson

A precious, mouldering* pleasure 't is
To meet an antique book,
In just the dress his century wore;
A privilege, I think,

His venerable hand to take,
And warming in our own,
A passage back, or two, to make
To times when he was young.

His quaint opinions to inspect,
His knowledge to unfold
On what concerns our mutual mind,

The literature of old;

What interested scholars most,
What competitions ran
When Plato* was a certainty.
And Sophocles a man;

When Sappho* was a living girl,
And Beatrice* wore
The gown that Dante* deified.
Facts, centuries before,

He traverses familiar,
As one should come to town
And tell you all your dreams were true;
He lived where dreams were sown.

His presence is enchantment,
You beg him not to go;
Old volumes shake their vellum* heads
And tantalize, just so.

* **Mouldering** means to show decay or age.
* **Plato** was a Greek philosopher.
* **Sophocles** was a Greek dramatist and philosopher.
* **Sappho** was a Greek poet.
* **Beatrice** was Dante's lover.
* **Dante** was an Italian writer from the Renaissance who famously depicted heaven and hell in his writing.
* **Vellum** is a type of animal skin that's often used as a writing material.

Introduction

"Guest's 'Good Books' and Emily Dickinson's 'In a Library' positively personify books. According to both writers, books are friendly, comforting entities that offer their readers plenty of rewards for reading."

Theme/Paragraph One: Where Guest personifies books as being 'friendly', Dickinson turns them into wise old men ready to share their wisdom.

- Throughout Guest's poem, he personifies the books, stressing their positive qualities. At the beginning of the poem, he states that 'Good books are friendly things to own.' Indeed, this focus on the friendliness of books is a theme throughout Guest's poem and is reiterated at the ends of the first and second stanza. These books are not only patient ('they will wait') and calm, but they also offer companionship to their readers, as explained at the beginning of the second stanza: 'The fellowship of books is real.' The use of end-stopped lines throughout the second stanza cumulatively lists all the benefits of books, especially their respectful nature (for example, 'They won't disturb you at your meal') and how they can offer a form of solace to their readers ('They'll comfort you when you are ill'). [*AO1 for incorporating textual references to justify and support an interpretation. AO2 for close analysis of the author's use of form and language*].

- Moreover, Guest uses a consistent structure in 'Good Books', which is made of three eight-lined stanzas of an ABAB rhyme scheme. Whilst the rhyme scheme gives the poem a light tone that celebrates these gentle companions, the ordered structure captures how regular and constant books can be. Like books on the shelf, these stanzas are regimented and neat, two qualities that the books described also have. [*AO2 for close analysis of the author's use of form and structure*].
- <u>Pivot to comparison:</u> Where Guest's books are friends, Dickinson's tone is somewhat more respectful to these older figures. From the beginning of the poem, Dickinson explains how it is 'A precious, mouldering pleasure' to 'meet an antique book' – the adjective 'mouldering' notes how old these books are, which is picked up again by the adjective 'antique'. This continues in the personification of the second stanza, in which Dickinson describes how the book extends 'His venerable hand to take'. The adjective 'venerable' not only emphasises how old these books are, but also that readers should treat them with respect. [*AO2 for close analysis of the author's use of language*].

Theme/Paragraph Two: Although Guest explores how loving books are, Dickinson goes further in exploring how reading can transport readers to new worlds and different time periods.

- At the end of the second stanza of Guest's poem, he states how even when for books 'you've ceased to care / Your constant friends they'll still remain', with the

enjambment metamorphosing[4] the initially negative sentiment into something positive that explores how books will remain 'constant friends' to their readers. Indeed, the anaphora throughout Guest's poem of 'They' (and its variations) constantly focuses on the books and their various benefits. [*AO1 for incorporating textual references to justify and support an interpretation. AO2 for close analysis of the author's use of form and language*].
- <u>Pivot to comparison:</u> Dickinson goes a little further, however. For Dickinson, books allow her to explore a new world. The metaphor of the book being 'In just the dress his century wore' adds a suggestion of how realistic books can be: they add something real for their readers. Furthermore, Dickinson uses enjambment between stanzas throughout her poem to suggest how flexible and free books are: they allow their readers to move across worlds with ease. For example, as described in the third stanza, they open 'His quaint opinions to inspect' and 'His knowledge to unfold / On what concerns our mutual mind'. The adjective 'quaint' notes the age of these 'opinions', whilst the unencumbered enjambment 'unfold[s]' the thought into the next line, emphasising the sentiment of how free these ideas are. [*AO2 for close analysis of the author's use of form and language*].
- As Dickinson's poem continues, it references various figures from throughout history, including: Plato, Sophocles, Sappho, Beatrice and Dante. These figures represent a variety of literary genres and are from different time periods – together, they highlight the possibilities of reading. Furthermore, in the penultimate stanza, Dickinson writes about how

books can 'tell you all your dreams were true'. This characterises books as travelling story tellers, with a natural optimism emerging from the focus on 'dreams'. Finally, the metaphor 'He lived where dreams were sown' emphasises how books encourage our dreams to grow organically. No wonder that at the beginning of the final stanza Dickinson states 'His presence is enchantment', which carries connotations of magic, therefore hinting at the transformative power of books. [*AO1 for incorporating textual references to justify and support an interpretation. AO2 for close analysis of the author's use of language*].

Conclusion

"As Dickinson's and Guest's poems demonstrate, reading is a gift. Not only does it, as in Dickinson, allow readers to travel to different places, but it also gives readers a friend for life, as in Guest. In the last line of Dickinson's poem, she uses the word 'tantalise', and that is just what a good book should do: give us just enough so that we're hungry for more."

NOTES

PAIRING I: WAR

1. Similes are comparisons that make use of either the word 'as' or 'like.'
2. You'll notice that I talk about word connotations a lot. This means when you explore specific ideas or emotions that come to mind when you read a particular word. These connotations are important – to say the wind was 'howling' is very different to say there was a 'gentle breeze'. Exploring word connotations is an effective method of language analysis and it's a brilliant way of expanding your vocabulary (which you can then use in your own creative writing endeavours during the English Language exams).
3. If something is **withered**, it is dry and shrivelled.
4. If something is **cumulative or building cumulatively,** it is increasing in quantity with each successive point.
5. When something is **amplified,** it is enlarged or increased (the word often applies to sound, but can be used here).
6. If something is **vivid,** then it produces a clear and powerful feeling in the reader's mind.
7. A **motif** is a recurring or reappearing idea in a piece of literature or art.
8. If something is **graphic**, then it's giving clear or vivid details.
9. When something is **visceral**, it's referring to bodily functions and so is quite gruesome.
10. At the **culmination** of something, it's reached its climax or conclusion.
11. To **dilute** something means to make it weaker, often by adding water.
12. An apostrophe is a figure of speech in which a thing/place/idea/person is addressed as if present and able to understand.
13. Obviously at this point I'm repeating much of the opening points of my Part a answer – this is absolutely fine and the exam board state that you can re-use material.
14. **Incessant** means to continue without pause or interruption.
15. If you're going to talk about rhyme, always draw explicit attention to **which** words rhyme – it makes it just that little bit clearer for your examiner.
16. When something is **insurmountable** it's too great to overcome.
17. The **domestic** refers to the running of the home or of family relations.
18. A couplet refers to a pair of lines in poetry/verse that often rhyme.
19. A **rudder** is a blade that goes at the back of a boat and is used for steering.
20. A metaphor is a linguistic device in which one thing is implicitly compared or likened to another thing. It is similar to another technical device we have

already encountered, the simile, which is when one thing is explicitly compared to another using the word 'like' or 'as'.

Let's briefly look at the difference between the two.

If I were to say: 'The pain felt like fire coursing through my body', this would be a simile, because I am using the word 'like' to compare my pain to fire.

However, if I were instead to say: 'The pain was a fire coursing through my body', this would be a metaphor. I'm still likening my pain to fire, but this time I'm not using the word 'like' and 'as' to make that comparison explicit.

Technically speaking, a simile is a type of metaphor, but for the sake of your GCSEs, it is best to think of them as two separate entities.

21. Anaphora is when the same word(s) are used at the beginning of successive clauses or sentences. As with all repetition, it's good to explicitly state which words are repeated for clarity.
22. Enjambment is when a thought/idea/sentence runs from one line of poetry into the next.
23. **Disparate** means that two things are so different, they cannot be compared.
24. If something is **perilous**, then it is full of danger or risk.
25. You'll notice I'm often stating **where** in the poem my quotes or details are from. Maintaining this clarity is really helpful for your examiner as it's easy to get lost in the specific details when analysing a text.
26. One translation of this Latin phrase might be: 'How sweet and fitting it is to die for one's country.'

PAIRING II: DEATH

1. In a world before mobile phones, telegrams could be sent over long distances. Using Morse code, which was translated by an operator, the messages were quick if brief (you're charged by the word when sending a telegram).
2. Notice how I don't give loads of historical information about the Boer War – it's just a polite nod to this reference and before moving back to the poem and its potential message.
3. **Evocative** means to bring forward strong images, feelings or memories.
4. The word '**tawny**' refers to an orange- or yellow-brown colour.
5. If you've got a feeling of **foreboding**, it means you've got the feeling that something is going to go wrong.
6. A euphemism is when something offensive or unpleasant is described in a way that is indirect, inoffensive or innocuous. For example, we might say someone was 'let go' instead of being fired – the former phrase is more polite and not quite as harsh as the latter.
7. **Ellipses** are a series of dots that indicate either the omission of a word or a pause.

8. If something is **pervasive**, it means it has been spread widely.
9. **Pathetic fallacy** is a type of personification where human emotions are given to inanimate objects in nature.
10. Always get the key term of the question into your essay early on so that it's clear to the examiner that you're focused on the **specific** topic you've been asked to write about.
11. **Elegiac** refers to an elegy, a type of poem that mourns the dead. To say something is elegiac, then, means it is sombre of tone and often sad at what has been lost.
12. Foreshadowing is a hint or warning of what is to come in the future; in a text, it is included by the narrator.
13. If something is **fragile**, it means it is easily broken.
14. For those of you who do not play *Call of Duty*, friendly fire is when you are hit during a battle by weapons from your own side.
15. **Parenthesis** is a remark/afterthought that is added into a sentence through brackets, commas or dashes, often providing extra information and/or an explanation.
16. **Caesuras** are a break/pause in a line of poetry.
17. An **annal** is a record of events in that particular year (annals will be arranged by year so you can use them easily to research).
18. Personification is when a writer gives human qualities to inanimate objects.
19. **Pastoral** refers to a genre that focuses on the lives of shepherds; it is an idealised, peaceful world surrounded by nature (which we might also call an **idyllic**).
20. **Depravity** suggests moral corruption and wickedness.

PAIRING III: LOVE

1. **Hypophora** is a rhetorical technique in which a rhetorical question receives an automatic answer.
2. A **sonnet** is a fourteen line poem, made up of an **octave** (the first eight lines) and a **sestet** (the remaining six lines). The switch from the octave to the sestet is called the ***volta***. Sonnets have different rhyme schemes depending on the type of sonnet (there's Petrarchan sonnets and Shakespearean sonnets, to name two, but there are others).
3. To **elope** means to run away and get married secretly.
4. If a text is **autobiographical**, then it has been written by the writer about their own life.
5. **Salvation** is the process of being saved from harm.
6. Being **virtuous** means having high moral standards.
7. To offer someone **consolation** means to give them comfort, often after a loss or disappointment.
8. If someone is being **oppressive** then they're cruel and unfair.

9. Notice here how I quote the repeated lines – whenever you write about repetition, be it normal or anaphora (see footnote 2 on page 185), always pop a quotation into your sentence, be it imbedded as above or in brackets/parenthesis so that it's clear what word you're referring to.
10. When something is **hypothetical**, it's based on a theory or idea.
11. Offering someone **solace** means to give them consolation (see footnote 7 on page 185).
12. To be **patriotic** means to be rigorously devoted to your country.
13. **Polyptoton** is a form of repetition in which the same word appears in different cases.
14. **Bounteous** means to generously provide for those who need it.
15. Being **zealous** means to show zeal (or passion) for a particular topic.

PAIRING IV: RELATIONSHIPS

1. To be **cynical** means to believe that people are motivated out of self-interest; more broadly, a cynical person is often distrustful of sincerity.
2. Shrek said it best when he observed how onions have layers, just like ogres. Although, in writing this footnote, it occurs to me that the first Shrek film came out in 2001, which would have been before you, dear reader, were born. Give me a minute whilst I go and lie in a darkened room.
3. An extended metaphor is, well, what it sounds like: a metaphor that goes across several stanzas of or the entirety of a poem.
4. To be **mundane** is to be dull.
5. An **entity** is a thing with a distinct independence and existence.
6. **Bathos** is a sudden change in subject, often moving from a serious to a trivial or ridiculous tone. But note how I define this unusual term within the body of my essay anyway, just so that the examiner is aware that I know what I'm talking about and not using fancy words incorrectly.
7. When something is **trivial**, it has little value or importance.
8. **Consumerism** focuses around the idea that happiness can be linked to material goods and possessions.
9. A dramatic monologue is a poetic form in which the imaginary speaker addresses an imaginary audience.
10. An **imperative** is a command.
11. When something is **subverted**, its power and authority has been undermined.
12. When a poem is written in **free verse**, it has no regular metre, rhythm, line length or rhyme.
13. If someone is **coy**, they're shy and bashful, with the hope of being attractive.
14. When someone is **vapid**, they're bland and not stimulating.
15. A **blazon** is a literary technique in which the writer catalogues an address.

16. To be **licentious** means to lack moral restraints, often sexually (ask your parents for more details).
17. **Discerning** something means to recognise it or to work it out.
18. Being a **materialist** means to be obsessed with physical objects or possessions.
19. Being **vacuous** means to show little thought or intelligence.
20. A **veneer** is a thin piece of decoration that covers over something more coarse and unsightly.
21. When commenting on a rhyme scheme, always write it out – as always, it just makes it clearer for your examiner.
22. Being **rakish** is to not have the best reputation, often because of previous naughty exploits.
23. When something or something is **unaffected**, then they're showing no signs of change.
24. To be **versatile** means to be able to adapt to different situations.
25. An **infatuation** is to have an intense, but often short-lived, admiration of someone or something. We've all been there, whether it be for a person or for a new song.
26. Notice how in this sentence I've managed to slip in some word analysis – connotations offer an easy way of picking up some analysis marks, so make sure you comment on them during your work.
27. If something is **potent**, then it'll have great power or influence.

PAIRING V: MARRIAGE

1. When someone is **mischievous**, they're often playfully naughty. This is a good example of where a choice adjective that summarises the speaker (or character, if discussing a play or novel) can really show your knowledge of the text.
2. When something is **overt**, then it's done openly.
3. A **sentimental** person often has feelings of tenderness and nostalgia.
4. A **flippant** person is someone who shows little respect.
5. An **evocation** is the act of recalling a feeling or memory.
6. **Chivalry** refers to the code of conduct that dictated those living in the medieval period.
7. A person who's **suave** is charming and confident.
8. If someone is **facetious**, then they joke inappropriately.
9. **Liquorice** is a chewy sweet with a strong taste.
10. When something is **clandestine**, it's being done secretively.
11. **Disenchantment** is a feeling of disappointment about someone or something.
12. If something is done **wistfully** then it has a feeling of regret and longing.
13. I used this quotation in the conclusion of my first answer, and now I'm using it early on in this answer. Remember, it's fine to re-use material, **but**

always try to frame it differently, just for variety.
14. It's absolutely fine to acknowledge that a line can have two meanings – it should show you're alert to the variety of ways literature might be read. Remember, any way is valid as long as the evidence you provide supports the point made.
15. To be **misogynistic** means to be prejudiced against women.
16. Again, the same point from before, but this time I'm using a different quotation.
17. A **reminiscence** is a story about a past event.
18. To be **wanton** means to be deliberately cruel, but often in an unprovoked way.

PAIRING VI: INNOCENCE

1. To feel **nostalgic** means to think positively about the past.
2. When something is **encroaching**, it is gradually moving across the accepted limits.
3. **Rapture** is an extreme, overwhelming state of positive emotions.
4. Do check footnote 6 on page 187 for a definition of chivalry and medieval courtly culture.
5. When something is **encapsulated**, it means the essential features are presented in a compressed way.
6. I've used brackets here to specifically quote the word that carries the connotations of delicacy.
7. Epic poetry is one of the oldest forms of poetry that's traditionally based on Greek and Roman history and mythology.
8. **Introspection** means to internally examine one's mental and emotional processes.
9. To **interject** means to say something abruptly.
10. When something (or someone) is **repellent**, then it means it causes disgust or pushes something else away.
11. Remember from our previous work on sonnets that a volta is a shift or change in a poem.
12. Exploring the themes seen in a writer's work is a useful way of writing about context.

PAIRING VII: PLACE

1. When something is **chartered**, it's formally written down (once the boundaries are established, it cannot be changed).
2. **Manacles** is another word for chains.
3. When exploring stanza lengths, especially if they're of different stanza lengths, it's good to state directly how long they are.

4. **Pessimism**, like cynicism, means to see the worse in people or believe that the worst will happen.
5. **Apocalyptic** refers to the end of the world.
6. To be **tentative** means to not be certain.

PAIRING VIII: NATURE

1. Once you've **reconciled** yourself to something, you've accepted it.
2. See footnote 11 on page 185.
3. If something is versatile, it means it is able to adapt and change.
4. A **slant rhyme** is where words have similar, but not identical, sounds (often called half rhymes).

PAIRING I: DREAMS

1. **Sustenance** is another word for food and drink that provides a source of strength.
2. When someone's **feeble**, they're weak.
3. **Respite** is a period of rest from something that's been difficult or exhausting.
4. When something is **ideological**, it's related to a set of ideas.

PAIRING II: LOSS/SADNESS/ISOLATION

1. **Lethargy** refers to having a lack of attention.

PAIRING III: LONDON

1. When something is **dour**, it's gloomy in its appearance.
2. **Morose** refers to a sad and sullen personality.
3. You might be unfamiliar familiar with the phrases 'iambic' and 'trochaic'. Let me explain.
   An iamb is a metrical foot in which the emphasis is on the second syllable, and tends to sound more like natural speech. It is often easiest to illustrate with an example. If we take the third line of Iris Tree's poem, and use bold font to represent the stressed syllables, plus a vertical bar to indicate the end of each metrical foot, it will look like this: 'To **watch** | her **moods**'. We have two iambic metrical feet in a row here, and thus line three is iambic.
   A trochee, on the other hand, is a metrical foot in which the emphasis is on the first syllable, and tends to sound more unnatural. To illustrate, let

us look at the fourth line in Tree's poem, and mark out the stresses on syllables: '**Wear**ying | **with** her'. As you can see, both feet have their stress on the first syllable as opposed to the second, and thus line four is trochaic.

The process of figuring out the metre of a poem is known as scansion, and it is not an exact science. For instance, some might argue that in line four of Tree's poem, we would also put a stress on the word 'her'. A metrical foot in which both syllables are stressed is known as a spondee. If we were to accept this argument, line four would then be a trochee followed by a spondee as opposed to two trochees.

4. **Nocturnal** refers to the nighttime.

PAIRING IV: BOOKS AND READING

1. **Affable** means to be friendly and personable.
2. **Congenial** refers to a person being pleasing.
3. **Fidelity** refers to someone being faithful.
4. **Metamorphosis** refers to a process of change.

Printed in Great Britain
by Amazon